CINEMAS OF NEWCASTLE

The Scala, Chillingham Road, 1936.

CINEMAS OF NEWCASTLE

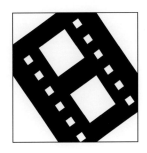

Frank Manders

Tyne Bridge Publishing

For Greta

This book is a revised and extended edition of *Cinemas of Newcastle* by Frank Manders published by Newcastle City Libraries and Arts in 1991.

Illustrations are part of the collections of Newcastle Libraries unless otherwise indicated.

For author's acknowledgements see page 164.

© Frank Manders, 2005

ISBN: 1857951522
Published by City of Newcastle upon Tyne
Newcastle Libraries & Information Service,
Tyne Bridge Publishing, 2005

www.tynebridgepublishing.co.uk

Tyne Bridge Publishing
City Library
Princess Square
Newcastle upon Tyne
NE99 1DX

Printed by Elanders Hindson, North Tyneside

Front cover: The Paramount, 1938.
Back cover: the Tyneside Cinema, 2004 (*Tyneside Cinema, David Williams*).
Inset: A Paramount usherette shows off her daring uniform in 1931 (*Mrs Muriel Bell*).

Selig's 'masterpiece of animal realism', The Lost City, as featured in the local trade magazine Northern Lights, 1920.

Main attractions

Supporting Programme

The Paramount advertises its forthcoming features, July 1933.

Introduction

In 1991 the first edition of *Cinemas of Newcastle* was published. Since then the whole experience of 'going to the pictures' has totally changed, and with the closure of the Odeon, Pilgrim Street, in November 2002 there are now no links in the city with cinema-going as it was for most of my lifetime. Gone forever are the local ownership of cinemas, the continuous performances, the Monday change of programme, the usherettes, the family audiences, above all the individuality of each venue.

Of course, as with most exercises in nostalgia, we forget the tatty rat-and-bug-infested fleapits full of cigarette smoke. We remember the great films of past decades while forgetting the shorts, the 'news magazines' and the awful second features that had to be endured before the main feature was reached. The old system was a world which was dying on its feet, having totally failed to keep pace with what the majority of the cinema-going public wanted from its cinemas. What contemporary audiences (now largely confined to one age group) want is clearly being provided by the multiplexes as cinema attendances increase year after year (although 2003 saw a dip for the first time since 1998).

A safety curtain hides the Paramount screen, 1931.
(Northumberland & Newcastle Society)

Although this book looks very different from the first edition, most of the text is basically the same, rearranged chronologically to tell the story in a more rational way. Much of the technical information in the first edition has been transferred to the 'supporting programme' on pages 155-163, while some of the longer descriptions of individual cinemas have gone altogether. In this new edition I have tried to put the emphasis on the cinema as part of the social history of the city and its people.

No new interviews have been undertaken for this edition, though I have included new information derived from continuing research. Much of Chapter 12 is new to the book: versions of some of it have been presented at a Mercia Cinema Society conference at Loughborough in 1993 and published in *Cinema Review*. It seemed helpful to say something about the way films found their way into cinemas and the complex local structures which once supported the industry, and of which there is now little trace.

Urbanora at Olympia, Northumberland Road, December 1905.

1 Before the cinemas 1896-1907

'THE CINEMATOGRAPHE. What in the world is it?' asked *Northern Gossip* on 28 March 1896. Its reply was: 'A series of instant snapshot photographs of a living scene are taken with such rapidity … that all the varying successive phases of the movement of a crowd, the actions of men at work, the restless motion of the sea, &c., &c., are faithfully recorded for all time. Photographs taken at the rate of 900 per minute. As taken they are thrown on the screen by electric light. Everything perfectly natural. The latest and greatest triumph in photography.'

A rather more coherent account had appeared in the *Newcastle Daily Chronicle* two days earlier: ' … the photographs, in their proper order, are made into a long band, which is passed rapidly through a lantern, the pictures being thrown in quick succession upon a screen. Owing to the circumstance that the retina of the eye retains its impressions of images, the rapid passage of the pictures gives the appearance of continuity, so that one sees the motions reproduced with life-like vividness.'

What these two reviewers had seen and were trying to explain was the first showing of moving pictures in Newcastle, at the Palace Theatre of Varieties in the Haymarket, on Thursday 26 March 1896. Performances were given for the rest of the week and for the whole of the following week. The Palace's main rival, the Empire Theatre of

"One Good Turn Succeeds Another."—Northern Gossip.

PALACE THEATRE OF VARIETIES,
HAYMARKET, NEWCASTLE-ON-TYNE.

"Hereto the tide of favour takes its way."—Northern Gossip.

This Commodious Theatre has been Reconstructed, handsomely Redecorated, Elaborately Upholstered, and Magnificently Lighted by Electricity, and is acknowledged to be the Favourite Place of Amusement in the City.

- - - - SPECIAL NOTICE - - - -

Ten of Thousands every week witness the Marvellous and Unparalleled Performances at the Palace Theatre.

THE ORIGINAL
CINEMATOGRAPHE,
THE MARVELLOUS
CINEMATOGRAPHE,
THE WONDERFUL
CINEMATOGRAPHE,
AT THE
PALACE THEATRE OF VARIETIES,
IS THE GREATEST OF ALL INVENTIONS.

THE CINEMATOGRAPHE,
The Wonder of the World. The Rage of London.
In addition, a Brilliant Array of Star Artistes.

THIS WEEK, commencing MARCH 30th,

WOOD & BEASLEY.	THE WEIMARS.	TOM GRAHAM.
SISTERS WYNNE.	CLIO & ROCHELLE.	BANCROFTS.
LIZZETTE TROUPE.	BELLA RUBINA.	BLACKHAM.
BROS. LANG.	THE DENNISONS.	AMY VICTOR.
TESSIE VANDEAN.	LOUIS PARVO.	GERTIE CORRIE.

Box Office Now Open.
Boxes, 2/6; Stalls & Centre Circle, 1/6; Circle, 1/-;
Pit, 6d.; Gallery, 4d.

The first cinematograph show at the Palace Theatre, March 1896.

Varieties in Newgate Street, also advertised the cinematograph for Saturday 28 March and the next week.

Five weeks earlier, the first public exhibitions of the cinematograph had been given in London, by the Lumière Brothers at the Polytechnic Hall, Regent Street on 20 February and by Robert W. Paul at Finsbury Technical College on the same day. Both shows transferred to variety theatres in London a few weeks later. This new form of entertainment arrived in Newcastle on 26 March, bypassing much larger cities further south. Where did the two rival projectors come from? Pre-publicity in the local press claimed that both shows were of the original Lumière Cinematographe (and even used the text of Lumière's London press releases), though neither was. The Palace Theatre's then managing director was Thomas Barrasford, who is known to have had an early interest in the medium. The projector could have been the French-made Kinetographe de Bedts (patented in Britain in March) or it could have been one of Robert Paul's machines, which he was selling by this date. The show at Richard Thornton's Empire Theatre, which claimed to be the 'First Appearance in the Provinces' was definitely given by a rather dodgy showman called T. Moore-Howard, possibly using a 'borrowed' projector made by a true pioneer such as Birt Acres or Robert Paul.

The films that were shown at the Palace and the Empire are less of a mystery: most can be identified as Edison Kinetoscopes (films made for peep-show machines), with titles such as *Cats dancing* and *Acrobat turning somersaults*. Each film, only about 50 feet long, lasted a few seconds. The *Newcastle Daily Journal* hoped that the cinematograph would be 'worked to better advantage shortly, for the vibra-

tion [flicker] noticed in all the scenes … was somewhat unpleasant to the eyes.' Consequently, apart from the press comments quoted earlier, there seems to have been little public reaction to this new form of entertainment and no apparent realisation that this was the beginning of something that for many people would revolutionise the use of leisure time.

Later in 1896 Newcastle audiences saw the best moving pictures then available. First came the original Cinematographe Lumière from the Empire, London, under the direction of Monsieur Trewey, a stage illusionist who handled the brothers' English interests. This headed the bill at the Empire Theatre in the week commencing 15 June. According to *Northern Gossip*, the pictures

… made quite a sensation. Chiefly through Mr Thornborrow's splendid arrangements, all the figures were perfectly clear and distinct. The whole 'show' was a touch of realism that interested and delighted … a boat rowed over sea breakers was exceedingly natural in all its movements, as also was the scene of workmen taking down a building. Everyone who has not seen this wonderful instrument should make an effort to do so this week.

On 2 November 1896 it was the turn of the English inventor, Robert Paul; the Empire Theatre was again the venue. Paul had the idea, followed by most proprietors of travelling picture shows, of filming locally. So, in addition to the famous film of the Prince of Wales' horse, Persimmon, winning the Derby, Newcastle audiences saw *Newcastle United Football Team at Play*, *Grainger Street at Noon*, and *Call Out of the Newcastle Fire Brigade*. The Palace Theatre replied with J. and F. Downey's 'Living Photographs', the 'Greatest Invention of the Nineteenth Century.'

From 1896 on, though moving pictures headed variety theatre bills, they drew decreasing attention from reviewers and were seen by some as a gimmick or passing fad. Even the first exhibitions in Newcastle of colour films, at H. Engel's Electrical Exhibition in the Art Gallery Theatre (Central Arcade) on 1 March 1897 and at the Palace Theatre on 3 May, with the new French invention, the Heliochromoscope, aroused relatively little attention.

Although in the next few years various moving picture shows – the Edison Vitagraphe, the Biograph, the Royal Vitascope, Gibbons' Bio-tableaux – continued to appear at the Empire and Palace Theatres, what enthusiasm there had been had

The Palace Theatre, Haymarket, on the corner of St Thomas's Street, 11 July 1906. The occasion was a royal visit.

clearly waned. Experiments were tried of incorporating the bioscope in regular attractions: the Vitagraph was used in the Palace Theatre's 1898 pantomime *Babes in the Wood* 'in place of the obsolete Harlequinade.'

With theatres losing interest, moving pictures were kept in the public eye by the travelling showmen; in Newcastle, those pioneers who hired public halls to give their entertainment were the most significant. The first of these was Charles W. Poole whose Myriorama shows had been travelling the country since the 1860s. The Myriorama was a series of huge painted canvases which, backlit, were moved across the stage between vertical rollers, while music played and lecturers interpreted the travel or historical scenes. In Poole's Christmas show at Olympia in 1897-98 was an innovation, the 'Eventographe', which was a true moving picture, the 'finest and steadiest' yet seen in the city.

In June 1897 the Modern Marvel Company's Analyticon (or stereoscopic projection) – the stereoscopic items were in fact slides, not films – visited the Grand Assembly Rooms, Barras Bridge. The Town Hall was also hired (by Livermore's Living Pictures in 1904 and New Century Pictures in 1905) as was the Exhibition Hall in St Mary's Place (by the New Bioscope Company, 1907).

The atmosphere of some of these travelling shows was described in *Northern Lights* in February 1920:

I well remember visiting a show of this kind when the pictures were the latest novelty out. The showman had … the hall fitted up with beautiful wooden forms, as hard as proverbial bricks, there was no operating box, no electric light, and no fine organ or orchestral accompaniment. The illuminant for this special performance was lime-light, as used in the oldest form of picture entertainment, the magic lantern. The show started about 8 pm, and as animated pictures were the latest boom the hall was packed at 1s. to 3s. a seat …

The company composing this particular entertainment I am thinking of was as follows: the showman, who was also the manager, operator, advertising manager, fly-poster, elocutionist and ventriloquist and anything else he could find time to do. His wife, who was also soprano vocalist, soubrette, and dancer, cashier and occasionally worked the lantern. These two together, with the lantern, the accompanist, and two local check-takers, gave an excellent programme, and it was worked after this manner.

First item, picture; second, illustrated song by the soprano vocalist; … third, another picture; fourth, a recitation to slides by the operator; … next item, another picture, and then ten minutes interval. … the show finishes on a comic picture, and everyone in those old days goes home pleased.

The home of the best travelling shows, a far cry from that just described, was Olympia in Northumberland Road. Opened in December 1893 as a general purpose hall, its promoters included H.E. Moss and Richard Thornton, who ran a chain of variety theatres. The hall was of corrugated sheeting on a cast iron framework, with an ornate plaster frontage. There were seats for 3,500. Olympia was frequently the venue for bioscope shows between 1897 and 1901. Its owners used it as a replacement while their new Empire Theatre was built in 1902-03 and when the latter opened, Moss and Thornton leased Olympia to Ralph Pringle, on condition that no variety acts would be staged there.

Pringle's North American Animated Picture Company

began a season at Olympia on 14 September 1903. The programme contained ten items, including colour films, with interludes by a military band and the band of the Wellesley Training Ship. There was one evening performance at 8 pm, with matinées on Wednesday and Saturday; prices were 3d to 2s. Pringle was followed by Waller Jeff's New Century Pictures:

> The pictures are certainly admirable, being the steadiest and best selected ever seen in Newcastle, those of local interest being exceptionally well received ... while those showing various incidents in a voyage across the Atlantic ... with sports on deck, and a most realistic representation of a storm in mid-ocean, were responsible for a tremendous outburst of applause.

Many shows of this type contained highly popular local films shot by Mitchell and Kenyon. People loved to see themselves on the screen in these 'local films for local people'.

In March 1904 the agreement not to stage variety was broken by Thornton himself and Sidney Bacon who opened the Olympia as a variety theatre with Lindon Travers as manager. Thus the claim made for Olympia that it was the first permanent cinema in the provinces, is ill-founded. The bioscope was soon back, however: in June 1905 the USA and Greater Britain Animated Pictures began a long season until September. One of this company's programmes contained 35 items, an indication of the abbreviated length of pictures at this period.

The greatest bioscope show at Olympia was undoubtedly the long season, beginning on 16 October 1905, of cinema

Urbanora at OLYMPIA.

Mr. C. RIDER-NOBLE, Manager.

Commencing MONDAY, OCTOBER 16th, 1905.

Every Evening at 8. Matinees—Wednesday and Saturday, at 3.
Doors Open Half-an-Hour Earlier.

Siege and Surrender of Port Arthur,

By permission of General's Nogi and Oshima

With Russian Army to Mukden,

By permission of General Kuropatkin.
The only Genuine War Pictures in existence.

ROMANCE OF THE RAILWAY,

Every Phase of its Construction and Working.

Motoring from Paris to Monte Carlo.

IMPERIAL BOYS' ORCHESTRA, 20 Instrumentalists,
Herr W. Linde, Musical Director.

ROYAL BEST, the World's Greatest Facial Expert.

Explanatory Lecturettes by LINDON TRAVERS, F.R.G.S.

PRICES.—Fauteils, Reserved, 2/-; Stalls and Balcony, 1/-; Amphitheatre, 6d. Children Half-price to all parts except Amphitheatre. Reserved Seats can be booked at Messrs. Alderson & Brentnall's, 125, Northumberland Street.

'Urbanora' at Olympia advertises in October 1905.

pioneer Charles Urban's 'Urbanora'. Urban and his local team took over the 'long neglected' Olympia, redecorated and reseated it and installed steam radiators to heat the huge hall. Employing a staff of 53, the company provided a superior product to the usual bioscope show. 'There have been many exhibitions of animated pictures, but those presented by Mr. Urban stand entirely on a different footing to anything yet shown here. The entire absence of flicker and the clearness of the pictures are two of their distinguishing features.' Also in the programme were 'chatty lecturettes' by Lindon Travers (grandfather of actor Bill Travers). It was Urbanora which staged the Blonde and Brunette Beauty Show in December, thought to be the first beauty contest in the country. The Urbanora season ended on 6 January 1906.

Olympia reverted to variety until the USA and Greater Britain company returned for a season in May-July 1906; it now advertised as 'The Home of Pictures'. In the early hours of 2 December 1907 it was totally destroyed by fire, the plaster frontage crashing into the street. But it had ensured that the moving picture had a future in Newcastle.

Testo's Royal Cinematograph booth at the Town Moor Hoppings, June 1908.

In contrast, the fairground showmen were of less importance. The first appearance of the bioscope on a Newcastle fairground seems to have been at Leazes in April 1898. Manders' Royal Waxworks and American Museum, open from 7 to 16 April, included 'the great cinematograph living pictures – the rage of the world.' The same show returned the next year from 30 March, advertising 'The freak museum of peculiar people and, just added, London's Latest Rage, the only Electric Cinematograph living pictures all worked by Electricity by means of a magnificent Engine.' As the years passed, many travelling bioscopes visited the Town Moor for the Hoppings, until put out of business by the permanent cinemas.

2 Testing the Water 1908

The city lost its premier venue for moving pictures when Olympia burned down in 1907, but it had shown by its success that there was a future for this still infant form of entertainment. In the course of the following year several individuals decided to try their luck as picture hall owners. Their approach was to alter existing buildings for cinema use rather than take the considerable financial risk of erecting purpose-built structures. By pure coincidence, in 1907 three branches of the Methodist Church amalgamated, making several church buildings redundant.

One of these was the former United Methodist chapel in Prudhoe Street, which became the Star Picture Hall; it opened on 13 April 1908 as the city's first permanent picture hall. It was owned by Audrey Appleby, whose USA Picture Company had given the last shows at Olympia. The building was altered very little inside or out; the horseshoe-shaped gallery was retained, though some sight lines must have been poor. The projector was on the floor of the hall, behind walls of three to four inch concrete. The arrangements were approved by *Northern Gossip* (which invariably gave a good review to any theatre or picture hall which paid for an advertisement): 'The beautiful surroundings, perfect attention and the conveniently serried rows of tip-up chairs make a visit to this place quite a pleasure.'

Almost 20 years later, an article in a national trade magazine mentioned that:

All manner of attractions were tried in those early days to popularise the picture entertainment, which was then regarded as a passing novelty, pleasing to the kiddies, may-be, but not likely to last long. Miss Appleby, for instance, used to hold periodical competitions in order to draw the crowds to see 'the flickers' as the films were often termed, and amongst those competitions were such gastronomic contests as devouring, against all comers, the largest number of raw onions, black puddings and white puddings. It is fearsome to look back and recollect how, in her hall, inflammable films running through an old-fashioned bioscope were no more than eighteen inches from a red-hot resistance, and, in the absence of take-up spool, then unknown, falling into a waste-paper basket, to be retrieved as might be, and rewound by hand. But the audiences of that time, mainly children, with few adults sprinkled about the hall did not realise the dangers they ran, and, therefore, thought nothing of them.

An advertisement of 1909 announces animated pictures at the Star Hall in Prudhoe Street.

In the early years at the Star there was an emphasis on locally-filmed events, like the Newcastle v. Wolves Cup Final in April 1908 and the Gosforth Park races in June. In January 1909, exclusive to the Star, were 'Talking and Singing Animated Pictures: the Latest Novelty: first time of this new principle in Newcastle.' Boxing films always appealed to early audiences: in March 1909 the Star had film, obtained at 'enormous cost', of the Johnson-Burns fight, which was run three times a day for two weeks.

In March 1911 Sidney Bacon took over the Star; it was to be reconstructed and redecorated on a 'lavish scale', with a new entrance from Northumberland Street (*The Bioscope*, 23 March 1911). This does not seem to have been done; Bacon let the hall to Edward Cant and John Grantham, who made minor alterations to the cinema in 1912-13 and replaced the tip-up chairs with forms. The Star, renamed the Apollo (possibly in May 1913), declined; it was no competition for the purpose-built cinemas now opening throughout the city. The Apollo appears to have closed in 1914; certainly in October W.H. Bacon of Olympia proposed to use the building as a 'Cinema Military Target Shooting Gallery', where potential soldiers could be trained. The hall was then used by Chapman's the furnishers.

Across Northumberland Street was the former Ginnett's Circus in Northumberland Road. Just over a month after the opening of the Star, Harry Taft leased the circus and opened it on 18 May 1908 as the Hippodrome, showing 'Animated Pictures of all Nations'. There was one performance nightly at 8 with special family matinées on Saturdays. Prices ranged from 3d to 1s, expensive for the period. On Friday 12 June there was a funny faces competition. This was thin fare with

The Apollo, Prudhoe Street, after closure c.1914. Note the performance times painted on the wall.

which to fill a large building and it closed as a picture hall on 18 June 1908.

In March 1909 another fly-by-night company took a lease of the premises and opened a picture show under the name of the New Olympia Animated Picture Co., offering twice nightly performances of 'The Finest Collection of Living Pictures' at a single price of one penny. The company, possibly operated by James Lowes (who had been involved with the Elswick) announced shows at this absurdly low price from 1 to 16 March, the local press claiming that their shows were 'up-to-date and enjoyable'. In their final advertisement the company said that it was 'a small advertisement but a big pennyworth' and stated that there would be 'No Fights', presumably meaning no boxing films would be shown (it is to be hoped that there was no fighting amongst the audience!). Although said to be 'drawing large crowds' on 9 March and meriting a review on the 16 March, the company then disappeared without further press comment. The Hippodrome was described as being in a dilapidated state in July 1909 ('most of the main supports are rotten, the whole building is bodily out of plumb, due to the prevailing westerly wind') and was demolished; the Olympia Picture Hall was built on its site.

The next picture hall to open was the Royal, in the Groat Market. The building had been a shop belonging to Ismay and Sons, wholesale chemists. The owners were the Royal Biograph Animated Picture Company, controlled by Jack Henderson, son of a film renter, who had run film shows at the Central Hall in Nelson Street, a temperance venue, from 2 January 1908 until the Friday before the Royal opened, 8 June 1908. The Henderson family were ardent temperance

The Royal: 'An up-to-date Picture Theatre in the Groat Market, and the pioneer of the Continuous Programme in the North of England'. From an advertisement in the Illustrated Chronicle, October 1912.

workers and since the beginning of animated pictures in 1896 Jack's father 'had hailed, with great pleasure, the advent of what he conceived to be a means of widening the scope, as well as extending the usefulness of Saturday entertainments for the people'.

In July 1908 the Royal showed a special film on the work of the Poor Children's Homes Association, which received the proceeds. In November, shows were run all day for the benefit of the large numbers of people in the city for the annual hiring of farm hands. In December 1908 an orchestra was introduced. As in most early picture halls, variety acts were part of the bill, for example 'Miss Maudie Sutton, catchy chorus singer, young and attractive' in March 1910. In February 1909 there was actuality film of the West Stanley pit disaster with a demonstration of the 'Draeger rescue apparatus'. Proceeds went to the disaster fund. Colour films were a feature of 1910 and the Royal appears to have been producing its own newsreel.

A raked floor was constructed in 1911. In October 1912, the Royal was the first Newcastle cinema to introduce continuous shows, abandoning twice-nightly performances, and by 1913 afternoon teas were being served to patrons in emulation of the grander cinemas then opening in the city. The Hendersons opened a small studio behind the Royal, where they produced, besides many local 'topicals' (news films), 'a film illustrative of a Tyneside poem, by Johnny Sands, with the well-known Tyneside comedian, J.C. Scatter, playing the dame, and Teddy P. Pirman the husband'.

So far, the three picture halls opened had been in the city centre. The first in the suburbs, opened on 20 July 1908, was the Tivoli at the corner of Walker Road and Raby Street in Byker. This was again a former United Methodist chapel and schoolroom. Edward Davison, who much later ran bingo at the nearby Raby, recalled the Tivoli at this period: 'For a while we [at the Raby] had a competitor called the Tivoli. It was an old building containing a large room. At the front was slung a white sheet and in the centre was a projector on a small wooden platform. The sheet would move with the draught and would often reveal the owner and his family sitting in front of an old kitchen range eating fish and chips.' The first owner was James A. Lauder, a stage conjuror; when he left to manage the New Empire (formerly Albert Hall) in Jarrow, the Tivoli had a succession of owners and managers. Matters were not helped by a fire on 15 April 1910 which damaged the stage area and destroyed the pianoforte.

The Tivoli was closed until early 1911; in the interim, architect J.J. Hill drew up plans to include a small stage and seating for about 250-300, with the forms at the front more expensive than those at the rear (in the early days, seats nearest the front were thought to be the best, as they were in the theatre). In February 1911 the cinema was being leased by a local company, grandly titled the British Canadian Animated Picture Co., with offices in Station Chambers, Neville Street and which also ran the Star, Easington Lane and the Central, Swalwell.

The Tivoli closed again, only to reopen under new management in July 1912 and was reported to be being 'going strong' in October, but it was probably the success of the purpose-built Raby which forced the closure of the Tivoli, as its operating licence was not renewed in December 1912. The building became part of a factory for Numol in 1919.

Next came the conversion of St Philip's Parochial Hall, at

The Tivoli, at the corner of Walker Road and Raby Street, August 1910.

the junction of Worley Street and Longley Street in Arthur's Hill. It first opened as the Imperial Picture Hall on 10 August 1908, managed by a Mr Tiplady; the large number of owners/lessees and names given to the venue before 1913 indicates a picture hall struggling for success. By December 1909 it was run by R. Piper and seated 420; the seating must have been chairs or forms on the hall floor. It next appears as Prince's Picture Hall in February 1910. In March 1910 the Crown Picture Co. reopened the hall as the Crown, run by a Mr Arkley (or Astley, or Artley!!): on 17 October it was taken over by Carl Aarstad of the Sun Picture Hall, Byker, who opened it as simply St Philip's Hall. Travel, dramatic, historical and comic pictures were promised. In a matter of weeks it was licensed to James Eadington and in 1911 was known as the Cosy.

The cinema appeared in its last incarnation in 1913 as the Stanhope Grand (though most people continued to call it the Cosy, which was certainly a more accurate name for a converted church hall). It was run from March 1913 until closure in 1931 by Joseph Broughton and William Revell Marshall. In June 1914 they installed a new projection box and in 1919 reseated the hall with tip-up chairs.

The Vaudeville in Church Street, Walker, was yet another chapel conversion. In February 1908 plans to convert the building into a theatre for W. Campbell-Maxwell of Wallsend had been initially rejected by the city council, but there must have been a change of heart, as on 9 November 1908 the Vaudeville was announced as opening shortly as a 'High Class Hall, Bioscope, Select Turns'. 'Rehearsals and artistes' trials' were advertised on 16 November and it opened on 23 November, with an emphasis on the 'turns'

(including 'Madame Tankerville, the celebrated operatic soprano') rather than the bioscope. After a brief reference in a trade magazine on 11 March 1909, when Frank Rowlands was manager, the fate of the Vaudeville was unrecorded until May 1910, when the city council approved plans for T. Proctor for a picture hall to seat a modest 360, all on the floor of the hall, with a shallow stage and space for a pianist or 'orchestra'. The hall was enlarged by incorporating into it former offices, passages and a yard at one side. 'The finest hall in the district' opened on 17 October 1910. The lessee was Arthur Sleep, who also ran the Tivoli, Spennymoor, and the projectionist was Percy Longhorn. (Percy Longhorn wore many hats: as a camera operator who filmed local newsreels for Henderson's the film renters, and who would photograph and star in what was apparently Newcastle's first feature film 'Mary and John', shot in the cornfields at Home Farm, Gosforth in September 1913. This film does not seem to have been completed. His family went on to own and operate the Orion, Westerhope.)

'The world's finest pictures' at the Vaudeville were supplemented by two variety acts, the '3 Royal Temples, Harmony Extraordinary' and 'Tiny Aston, the Wonderful Boy Actor/Vocalist.' Soon after opening, in November 1910, the Vaudeville put on a show for locked-out shipyard workers, with free tobacco; the resulting crowd had to be controlled by the police.

In June 1911 new owner T.M. Miller increased the picture hall's capacity to 390 by adding a small balcony reached by six steps from the floor of the hall. Ownership changed to William Baker in May 1912; he already ran the Gaiety, Newcastle, the Coliseum, Whitley Bay and the Empire,

Wheatley Hill. In about 1919 he was joined by his cousin Thomas Roche (of the Imperial, Tyne Dock). The Vaudeville was owned by the Baker family until closure.

Along Scotswood Road, the Elswick Picture Palace opened officially on 14 December 1908. This was the former New Tyne Circus which had become the Queen's Theatre on 12 November 1900. It appears to have closed in 1906 and in March 1908 the council rejected a proposal by William Dobie of Sunderland to convert the building to a picture hall.

Council officers must therefore have been surprised to read in the *Newcastle Daily Chronicle* on 9 November 1908 that the well-known publican and boxing promoter James 'Jimmy' Lowes had opened the theatre as the Newcastle Sporting Club and was running boxing contests and bioscope shows. The building must by now have been in a dilapidated state, but Lowes' patrons didn't seem to mind. By December 1908 the Newcastle Sporting Club was being advertised as the Elswick Picture Palace and 'has met a felt want in that locality. The entertainments have been well patronised…'.

The city council was naturally disturbed that a building which had been refused a licence 18 months earlier was still open and could hold 2,000 people. Correspondence ensued with Lowes in the course of which it transpired that 'the firm that is running the pictures is from London'. It was in fact the respected production company Walturdaw. As might be expected, the few available advertisements for the Elswick show a heavy emphasis on films of boxing matches. Beauty contests were also being staged: 'First prize – Guinea Hat. Second prize – Half-guinea Hat.' The decrepit Elswick Picture Palace closed on 16 January 1909.

The last of the city's seven picture halls of 1908 was the

The King's, Marlborough Crescent, February 1930.

King's Hall, Marlborough Crescent, opened on New Year's Eve in the former Drysdale Hall, latterly a Roman Catholic junior school. Interviewed in 1931, Joseph Collins, then northern district manager for Paramount, reminisced about

Newcastle Chronicle & Journal Ltd.

the King's Hall. He and his brothers, he said, had opened the King's as a picture hall in 1905. 'We had seen the "pictures" showing in shops in London and had come to the conclusion that there was a big future in the business … We owned the King's Hall for five years – five happy years they were with all the fun of a new enterprise about them. We then sold out to Mr. Jimmie Lowes and ourselves branched out into more ambitious enterprises'.

If Collins' memory was accurate this makes the King's the first permanent picture hall in Newcastle by a wide margin, but it seems unlikely that it was. The earliest newspaper advertisement traced was for the opening on 31 December 1908, and a management which subsequently advertised so aggressively would surely not have failed to do so had the hall existed earlier. In any case, on 4 November 1908, Jimmy Lowes had submitted a proposal to the city council for the conversion of the hall for boxing and pictures, presumably anticipating that the Elswick Picture Palace would be closed down. These proposals were rejected, but do suggest that Collins did not have any connection with the building until December 1908.

The King's ('The Cosiest Hall in the City') was opened on 31 December 1908, 'remodelled, redecorated, and reseated at enormous expense'. There were two performances each evening of 'superb pictures and high-class varieties'. There were waiting rooms for patrons and bicycles were stored free. In its first four years under Collins, the King's advertised widely in the press, with boasts of 'no intervals or weary waits' (presumably meaning a second projector had been installed) and 'no vulgarity or rowdyism at the King's'. There was also an obsession with music hall-style alliteration:

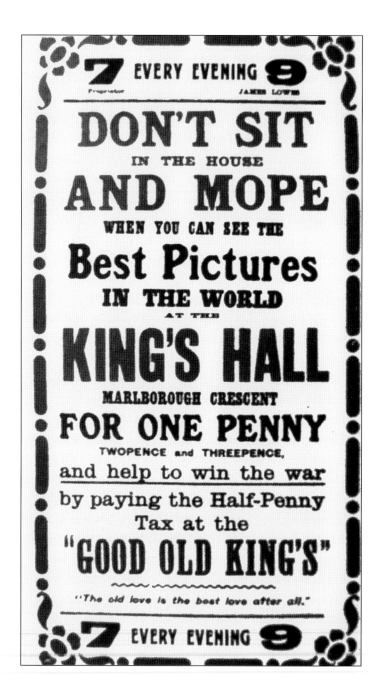

'Silent sensations and subdued symphonies in scarlet' (whatever that means), 'clever comedians, aristocratic actors, topical trips and tours'.

In December 1911 James Lowes took over the King's and, with his main interest being in boxing promotions, the cinema's advertisements became less self-confident and finally stopped. Lowes boasted in 1912 that the King's had 'no tip-up chairs' – presumably they had been replaced by benches so that more people could be crammed in. It became just another local cinema, drawing its audience from the crowded streets off Scotswood Road and Westmorland Road.

By the close of 1908, picture halls had firmly established themselves in the city. What sort of people had taken a chance and invested their money in the young business? Of the seven halls opened in the course of the year, three were owned by people with previous experience in the business: Audrey Appleby of the Star, John Henderson of the Royal and Joseph Collins of the King's. The latter two were also film renters. J.A. Lauder of the Tivoli was a stage conjurer, Jimmy Lowes of the Elswick a boxing promoter and property dealer. The trades or professions of the other two are unknown.

Three of the halls were converted from churches or church halls, two from circuses/theatres, one from a shop, and one from a school. Very little needed to be done in terms of building alterations: the churches especially were already designed to concentrate the audience's attention on a central focal point. In the Star the horseshoe-shaped gallery was retained; in the King's galleries were built along both side walls, reached by iron staircases. Most of the seating in these picture halls was on the flat floor, on chairs, wooden benches

Fire extinguisher advertised in Northern Lights, 1919.

or forms. Some halls used tip-up chairs, but these were not upholstered. These halls varied widely in audience capacity, from 360 at the Vaudeville to 1,250 at the Royal and possibly 2,000 at the Elswick. All opened for two separate shows in the evening, at 7 pm and 9 pm, with a matinée for children on Saturday afternoon. Admission prices were from 2d to 1s with half price for children.

The chief item of equipment necessary was the film projector. Although there was as yet no legislation governing its use, awareness of the flammability of nitrate film necessitated its separation from the audience, for example, behind walls of three to four inch concrete at the Star; in a brick projection box at the King's. Fiction films at this period were usually from 300 to 500 feet long, running for approximately 3-5 minutes each, so there was a great need for something to fill the periods when the single projector was being loaded. Variety acts or 'turns' also gave a change of pace to the evening's entertainment. Most picture halls had regular 'go-as-you-please' nights (performances by local talent), and amateur singing competitions.

3 The first wave 1909-1913

After December 1908, no picture halls opened in the city until the Sun at Byker Hill in November and the Olympia in Northumberland Road in December 1909. This absence of activity can only be explained by a cautious approach on the part of would-be picture hall proprietors, who wished to be assured that all the halls opened in the previous year were trading successfully and that this new form of entertainment had a future. As we have seen, only two of the seven failed, and these two were by far the most ramshackle. The time was therefore judged to be right for the building of picture halls as such rather than the conversion of existing buildings. In these new buildings, sight lines to the screen could be improved and floors raked.

The first of these purpose-designed picture halls was the Olympia, in Northumberland Road, opened on 20 December 1909. The trade paper *The Bioscope* noted:

> By the continual addition to the list of picture halls on Tyneside, it is evident that 'living' pictures continue to maintain their popularity ... Built on the site of Ginnett's Circus, accommodation is provided for 1,500 persons, and a sloping floor makes it possible for everyone in the hall to see every picture and artiste with the greatest ease. Erected of red pressed bricks with stone dressings, the building is undoubtedly an architectural adornment, while the most up-to-date apparatus is employed for showing the pictures to the best advantage.

The report went on to praise the amber-coloured lighting which made 'darkness visible', the cloak rooms and attendants and the tip-up seats. Indicating the new trend in the financing of cinema buildings, the Olympia was owned by the Northern Cinematograph Company. The roof of the hall was of corrugated iron sheeting, while inside the roof trusses were clearly visible. Internal walls were lined with wood and plaster.

At the opening performance, encores were demanded for some of the films, while music was provided by the Lovaine Quartette. Variety acts early in 1910 included 'Ada Cuffy, a real coloured lady' and Little Violette, a female impersonator. In March 1910 Sidney Bacon took over the cinema and appointed the popular lecturer Lindon Travers as manager. 'It will be the scene of perfectly appointed pictorial entertainments twice nightly, with vocal and orchestral concerts at popular prices and a complete change of pictures twice a week ...' Always advertised as 'Sidney Bacon's Olympia', 'pictures, music, order, comfort' were promised. By December 1910, Bacon offered a show where 'The Pictures are All New. Professional Orchestral Septette, Professional Management, and Auxiliary Staff of ex-Police and Military as attendants for the Comfort of Patrons.'

During the war the Olympia went over to continuous performances: the programmes were liberally dosed with come-

Sidney Bacon's Olympia, with the White City beyond, 1910.

dies and serials, staple suburban fare in a city centre cinema. Lindon Travers died in November 1918 and films became even less distinguished. With much competition in the city centre, films often reached the Olympia after suburban showings. Seat prices in the twenties and thirties were cheaper than when the cinema had opened.

Almost all the remaining picture halls of this period were built away from the city centre, in heavily populated urban areas, drawing their audiences from the closely packed terraced streets of the east and west ends. At the junction of Commercial Road and Oban Road, Byker, the Raby Hall was opened, probably on 17 January 1910. The angle of the two streets was acute, giving the picture hall a coffin-like shape. The original owners were Willis and Moffat, but in September 1910 it was acquired by Robert Scott, of 'Scott's Perfect Pictures' (who also had the Imperials at Dunston and Felling) showing 'best varieties and pictures'. In 1913 it was owned by James A Lauder, who had managed the Tivoli nearby in its early days. By 1917 it was run by Joseph Broughton and William R. Marshall, trading as the Castle Cinema Company. The Raby had a manageress, Mrs A.M.

Moffatt, from 1919 to 1923; this was rare in the city.

The Brinkburn in Brinkburn Street, Byker, was Wallsend builder James MacHarg's first picture hall in the city. It was opened on 25 February 1910 by an ex-Sheriff of Newcastle, Councillor Arthur Scott, who characterised picture halls as presenting great educational advantages to the people. The hall itself was an unadorned, functional building. Both stalls and circle had raked floors, and were seated with tip-ups, although in the stalls, the tip-ups were in lengths of 4 feet 6 inches. Only in the front circle were the seats upholstered (by Bainbridge's).

The Raby Picture Hall in 1910, showing the owners Messrs Willis and Moffat, in top hats. The man in the bowler is possibly their operator (projectionist).

Tony Moss

The Brinkburn was not without pretensions, advertising throughout 1910 as 'The finest theatre and pictures in the North'. Variety acts were prominent in the programme. There were the usual two shows nightly, prices ranging from 2d to 6d with half-price children's matinées every Saturday. Cycles, prams and go-carts were stored without charge. On some weeknights Boy Scouts in uniform were admitted free. On 27 November 1910 the Brinkburn promoted a concert under the chairmanship of James Lawrence of Newcastle United in aid of the East End Distress Fund.

The Brinkburn, 1957.

The first manager, George Edminson, stayed for the unusually long time of 12 years. There is perhaps a touch of the back-handed compliment in *Northern Lights'* remark that 'it says much for Mr Edminson's business acumen and forethought that he is still in the position where he started in 1910.' In 1920 the hall was redecorated 'in a very artistic manner' in cream and gold.

Not far away, on Byker Bank, the Minerva opened, probably on 15 August 1910. 'Acknowledged to be the prettiest theatre in the district' (advertisement, 1910), the Minerva was built by a private company with £2,200 in shares called Heaton and Byker People's Hall Ltd, formed in March 1910 by J. Dickenson, a Newcastle photographer and others. The hall was modest in size, seating only 360. From about 1911 to 1918 it was leased to Mr E. Pirman. Agnes Smurthwaite, reminiscing for the *Byker Phoenix* in July 1980, recalled: '…being taken to the Minerva to see silent films in 1913. The first owner was a Mr Purman [sic], and there was a three-piece orchestra … There would always be somebody who couldn't read who would sit beside [my] mother and ask 'What does it say?' One week a different picture was shown

The Imperial, 1925, pictured on a letterhead.

every night to packed houses.'

The Adelaide was Benwell's first picture hall, opening on 17 October 1910. At the corner of Adelaide Terrace and Maria Street, it was owned by a local fishmonger, W.H. Rewcastle. The small 21-foot stage had 'a tasteful proscenium' and the hall was heated throughout. The operator (projectionist) was John Grantham, the first public appearance in Newcastle of this future cinema owner and Lord Mayor. There was usually a variety act in addition to the films: the stage was enlarged in 1911.

Rewcastle made every effort to run a cinema which was a part of the community: something of this comes over in an advertisement from 1912:

When looking for enjoyment, combined with refinement, make a point of starting the New Year with being a regular patron of the ADELAIDE P.H., where you can find these features predominate. Our success has been attained by studying your requirements, and seeing that you get them. We have made thousands of friends, and are still friendly with them all. This alone speaks volumes for all of us.

Keytone Publications

Above, the Adelaide, c.1937.

Right, W.H. Rewcastle advertises his services in the trade magazine, Northern Lights, 1920.

W. H. Rewcastle

Requires the Management of a Cinema. Experienced both in Pictures and Variety.

A sure Money-maker.

Apply : 66, Hampstead Road, Newcastle-upon-Tyne.

The Adelaide auditorium, c.1937.

The Globe on Salters Road, Gosforth, was built by a syndicate led by Joseph R. Collins (of the King's, Marlborough Crescent) and was opened on 19 December 1910. It was agreed by the trade press to be the finest theatre yet built in the area, the first to have fireproof scenery and a safety curtain on the stage. The projector was motor-driven rather than hand-cranked, which was normal at this time. The construction cost was said to be over £12,000.

… the interior is luxuriously appointed, comfortable accommodation being provided for about 1,000 persons … A new feature, so far as picture theatres in the North is concerned, is the provision of several private boxes, and these are tastefully furnished in keeping with the remainder of the building … [A] high-class cinematograph and vaudeville entertainment will be given twice each evening and on Saturday afternoons.

The original plans of April 1910 show two billiard rooms in a basement: a 'select' room with two tables and a general room with six tables. These had been eliminated in the final plans of May. The cinema was actually licensed for 883. The stalls area, with tip-up seats, was priced from 2d at the front to 6d at the rear, each division separated by a moveable barrier; the balcony, seating 180, was 1s at the front and 6d at the rear; the operating box was behind it. The private boxes were at the rear of the stalls.

The success of the Globe is indicated by the fact that the manager was twice fined, in 1912 and 1913, for overcrowding [people standing in the gangways]. The cinema made a rather more dramatic appearance in the local press on 24 February 1913:

Early on Saturday morning an outrage by Suffragists was committed at the Globe Electric Theatre, Gosforth. The theatre had been let for the purpose of a political gathering in the afternoon under the auspices of the Gosforth and Coxlodge Liberal Association … The damage was discovered when the theatre was entered, and it was then ascertained that a plate-glass window in the foyer of the theatre, which was guarded by an iron gate, had been smashed. A hammer-head had been thrown through it, and this was found in the doorway. To the hammerhead was attached a label which bore the words 'Let fresh air into politics by votes for women'.

In February 1915 the Globe was taken over by Sidney Bamford who ran it almost to the end of the silent period, although the connection with J.R. Collins was retained. The programming during and after the First World War was good: the cinema was sufficiently far from the city centre to be able to present major features with comedy support and run them for a whole week. The variety acts were dispensed with during the war but reintroduced (on Tuesday and Thursday only) in the late twenties.

The Crown Electric Theatre was built on the site of the Elswick Picture Palace on Scotswood Road for Joseph Dobson, an auctioneer and house agent, opening on 24 December 1910. It is described in a national trade journal on 5 January 1911:

The Crown after fire damage in 1971.

> **Situated immediately facing a section of the famous Elswick Works of Sir W G Armstrong, Whitworth & Co., Ltd., a populous neighbourhood is to be served. Twice nightly and Saturday matinées are to be the rule, first-class features with vaudeville to be featured. The fine building seats 2,000, all in comfortable tip-ups … The whole of [the] seating forms a segment of a circle, and owing to great width and ample rake an excellent view is obtained from all parts …**

Like most local cinemas, the Crown management ran special events for its patrons: in April 1912 there was a seaside treat for the children of regulars. The Crown abandoned variety acts by 1914, one of the first cinemas to do so. At one period in 1915 it had the lowest adult seat price recorded in the city – 1½d . Occasionally a special picture, such as *The*

Rosary in 1916, was accompanied by an improving lecture.

The Grand Cinema Palace, to give it its original name, on Condercum Road, Benwell, was one of the city cinemas whose opening, on 7 August 1911, was recorded in the national trade press. *Kinematograph and Lantern Weekly* reported:

> **The opening of this handsome new theatre, designed by the famous firm of local architects, Messrs. Gibson and Stienlet, who have now quite a number of theatres to their credit, took place on Bank Holiday, two crowded audiences attending. The decorative scheme in crimson, white and cream is further enhanced by the beautiful plaster work on ceiling, walls and proscenium in Louis Quinze style, with fruit and flower festoons, this work by Anderson's of South Shields. A full stage, with beautiful**

The Grand, Condercum Road, Benwell, c.1929.

scenery by Albion Studios, Newcastle, calls for special comment, and is deservedly entitled to rank among the finest in the district; it is fully equipped for all vaudeville interludes, etc. … Current for the entire building and arcs, etc., is supplied by a large Siemens dynamo driven by a 16 h.p. Crossley engine. The lessees are Messrs. Jack Grantham, late of Hartlepool and Newcastle theatres, and Eddie Cant, late of Star Picture House and Sidney Bacon's Pictures, men with a sound exhibiting and mechanical training, who will fully gauge the public tastes… The building is being flanked on one side by a long verandah canopy for use of waiting visitors.

The Grand's power supply.

West Newcastle Local Studies

The following account, from *KLW* of 9 November 1911, is probably not typical, but is an example of the excitement (and noise) which could be generated by the 'silent' film and of the methods used in the early years to promote the product:

A series of packed houses marked the initial performances, under exclusive rights, of Rob Roy at the Grand Cinema, Newcastle … During the pictures, graphic Highland pipe effects were given by Pipe-Major Sutherland (late Seaforth Highlanders) and Sergeant Alec Marshall, drums also being employed in places. This alone aroused enthusiasm, but at the finale, when the screen disappeared and disclosed the famous Highland band of the Northumberland Veterans, under Drum-Major Bevan, the applause was greater still. Their fine display, with special lighting effects and stirring Scottish music, created a furore such as has never previously been witnessed in any local picture house. National dances by the smart Edina Troupe followed, to the great delight of the Scots present, then the grand finale by the full band closed what can only be classed as a really memorable performance.

A more typical vaudeville performance was advertised on 6 January 1912: 'Amases, the Egyptian Man of Mystery in a Wonderful Exhibition of Eastern Magic, also Frederica's

Wonderful Terriers and Cake-Walking Pony'.

The Brighton Electric Theatre, at the junction of Westgate Road and Lynnwood Terrace, was the first element in a three-phase 'leisure centre'. The cinema opened on 10 July 1911, followed on 2 November 1911 by the Brighton Assembly Hall, seating 800 and available for dances and other functions. These were followed on 4 April 1912 by a nine-table billiard hall. The whole complex was similar in concept to the Heaton at the opposite end of the city. The controlling company was Newcastle Entertainments Ltd.

The Brighton was licensed for 1,099, including 14 in four boxes, which were at the rear of the stalls; some were initially reserved for the directors of the company and their friends. The opening programme included the colour film *Aida*, an 'Egyptian drama', suitably accompanied by the Cairo Trio, 'Oriental musicians'. 'The building continually rang with expressions of appreciation'. In the early years, films were accompanied by 'Goffin's Bijou Orchestra (Finest in the North)'. Family ticket books, offering a saving on normal seat prices, were available and there was a children's matinée every Saturday.

Armstrong Electric Theatres

Ltd., a £4,000 company formed by J.P. Oliver, wine and spirit merchant, S.W. Wallhead, auctioneer, and others in November 1912, opened the Scala Electric Theatre at the junction of Chillingham Road and Tosson Terrace, Heaton, on 10 March 1913, at a time when there was much debate in the city about the growing number of cinemas. The picture hall owners were concerned that there were now too many cinemas in the city with a consequent danger that profits

The Brighton, 1912.

Tony Moss

The Scala, Chillingham Road.

might be spread too thinly. F.W. Morrison, a spokesman for local cinema interests, multiplied the seating capacity of Newcastle's four theatres, three music halls and 21 cinemas by the number of performances to demonstrate that there were 380,000 seats for a population of 277,000. On the basis of this dubious calculation, the city council was asked to refuse all future applications for cinema licences; this was not agreed. Alderman Arthur Scott, who formally opened the Scala, used the market forces argument in its support: 'It was said that Newcastle had too many such places …To his mind it was a question of supply and demand, and so long as there was a demand for picture halls they should be built.'

The Scala 'had a spacious tiled entrance, with marble staircases approaching the dress circle, and in the auditorium are three divisions, the pit, pit stalls and elevation. The total seating capacity, together with the four family boxes, is 1,200. The upholstering is of red plush … The proscenium has an opening 24 feet wide and 23 feet high, and there is a large stage with the usual dressing accommodation for artists.' The building was said to have cost £7,000. The fare at the Scala in its early years was the usual mix of pictures and variety; books of family tickets were available. The variety acts seem to have been dropped by 1914.

The Bamborough (or Bamboro', as it was often called) was at the top of Shields Road, at the junction of Union Road, Thornborough Street and Bamborough Street. It was owned for all its life by the Renwick family. The early years of this cinema are something of a mystery; no plan has been traced and there was no press report of its opening, which was probably on 16 July 1913. It seated about 675. The plans for the Bamborough had been passed by the city council on 5 February 1913 despite a motion that the proposed cinema was redundant (ie superfluous). The hall had its projection room at stalls level. The circle was reached by stairs on the left hand side of the foyer, while there was no false ceiling – the roof trusses were clearly visible. By the 1950s a ceiling of building board had been added.

In the years up to the First World War, those who wished to enter the cinema business but could not afford to finance a new building continued to convert existing premises. All over the country picture halls were being opened in converted

S.N. Wood

The Bamboro' after closure, 1964.

churches: the Sun Picture Hall, at Long Row, Byker Hill, was different. It had formerly been a slipper factory built in 1902; by 1909 it had closed and was converted to a picture hall for Carl Albert Aarstad, a Heaton merchant, who became lessee and manager. There was a small stage 12 feet deep and seating was 350. The Sun was formally opened on 29 November 1909: '... there was a crowded attendance. An excellent cinematograph machine has been installed, and a number of varied and interesting pictures delighted those present.' The main pictures were *Leather Stocking* and *The Airship*

John Airey

The Mechanics' Institute in Walker as 'The Walker Picture House' c.1910.

Destroyer. There was a performance by Miss Le Clair, 'the favourite vocalist'.

The first floor concert hall of the Walker Mechanics' Institute on Church Street had always been available for hire; on occasion to owners of travelling picture shows. It may have been in use as a picture hall in 1907: an advertisement for 'Joshua Dyson's Gipsy Choir, Dioramas and Animated Pictures' of January 1910 mentions a visit to the hall three years earlier. In February 1910 the city council passed a plan

for the addition to the hall of a 'fireproof chamber' (ie an operating box) for the committee of the Mechanics' Institute. The hall was licensed as a cinema on 1 April 1910; the licensee was John Brown and the name 'Favourite' was chosen, although the name board on a postcard of the hall about this time indicates that the building was known as the 'Walker Picture House'.

The Kinematograph and Lantern Weekly of 5 February 1911 reported:

Since taking over the fine Mechanics' Hall at Walker, which had the doubtful distinction before this of having changed hands about forty times in as many years, [the lessee James] Simpson has quite rejuvenated the place. Considerable expense was incurred in adapting and decorating the interior, but it was justified, takings improving week after week. Pictures of the best, interspersed with good turns, have had their effect, and now 'standing room only' applies almost nightly. On a recent date some 1,400 paid for admission to a charity show. Seating, however, is nominally for 850.

Despite Simpson's apparent success, he did not stay much longer: *Kinematograph Weekly* (11 May 1911) records that the Favourite Palace, Church Street, would be opened on 15 May by Marshall J. Rutter, of the Picturedrome, Newburn and the Palace, Horden. In 1912 a sloping floor was constructed and in 1913 the lease was transferred to John Scott, who stayed until 1923.

The Picturedrome, at the corner of Gibson Street and Buxton Street, was the least prepossessing of all Newcastle's cinemas. The building dated from 1878 and had been a large 3-storey house with shop premises on the ground floor. It opened on 30 July 1910 and was noticed by the trade magazine *The Bioscope*:

It comprises the site originally occupied by Mr. Harrison, draper … the new hall having seating accommodation for 450 to 500 patrons. [About 150 of these seats were in a gallery on the rear and side walls of the former first floor]. The floor has been provided with a good rake, so that a perfect view of the picture can always be obtained. George Besford, who owned the picture hall along with Hugh Millar, was chairman of the Northumberland and Durham Picture Hall Managers' Association, and was said in October 1912 to have 'received flattering reports from the authorities regarding the change which has come over the district since he opened'.

The Picturedrome was owned for all of its 50 years by the Millar family.

The Picturedrome, on the corner of Gibson Street, in its closing week, August 1960.

Newcastle Chronicle & Journal Ltd.

In November 1910, William Fenwick applied to the city council for a cinematograph licence for the hall of the Blaydon and District's Co-operative Society's premises on Denton Road, Scotswood. This society was keen to let its halls for picture shows, having had them at its Blaydon and Chopwell stores since 1909. The application for a licence at the Denton Road store was refused on 16 November because of lack of fire appliances. But despite this *The Kinematograph and Lantern Weekly* of 8 December 1910 reported that a Mr McAlistor had opened the store hall as a picture hall called the Electra. Despite there being no record of any alteration to the hall – the construction of a fireproof chamber for the projector, for example – the Electra continued to be reported as open until 12 January 1911.

The Gaiety in Nelson Street opened on 29 March 1911. The building had had a complicated history since opening as a music (i.e. concert) hall in 1838. By 1908 it was the Central Hall, a temperance venue which had hosted kinematograph shows by Jack Henderson in early 1908 and further picture shows were given there in January 1911 as part of temperance meetings. But as early as February 1910 R. & W. Baker had submitted plans to the city council to raise the floor of the Central Hall to give a rake, which suggests a permanent cinema show. In December 1910 the Baker brothers, with architect Percy L. Browne, submitted further plans for the full conversion of the hall to a cinema, to seat 528 in the stalls and 402 in the gallery. These plans were refused, but revised plans of January 1911 were passed, though the council clearly had doubts about the suitability of the first floor hall as a cinema. At the end of March the Gaiety Picture Hall opened. What seems to have happened is that the Baker brothers ran picture shows for the temperance committee, saw the commercial potential and persuaded the temperance people to leave – they went to a hall in Westgate Road.

The conversion was said to have cost several thousand pounds and the hall to seat 1,000 comfortably, but in fact it was licensed for only 875. The cinema retained its old concert hall appearance. It was on the first floor, above a fruit wholesaler's, with a tiny stage 25 feet wide and only 10 feet deep. The balcony extended along both side walls towards the proscenium arch.

The Gaiety offered 'high class variety' and pictures at two performances nightly with matinées on Wednesday and Saturday. On opening night:

> **… two packed audiences showed evident appreciation of the programme put before them and the arrangements made for their comfort. The pictures are steady and clear, the comic element predominating. Two very fine dramatic films were shown, together with a long one describing a trip through Holland** [that sounds exciting!] **… The Morellis present this week a clever and enjoyable musical act, the other turn being provided by a dancer of no mean ability.**

On Friday of the opening week a film of the launch of HMS *Monarch* from Armstrong, Whitworth's Elswick yard was shown, 'specially taken for Messrs, Baker Bros.'. There was a Thursday change of programme and seats were all tip-ups. By 1912 there was a 'Grand Orchestra' under the baton of Mr F. Young.

Variety performances ceased about 1915. Many of the

The Gaiety, Nelson Street, 1912.

films shown were British, from the Hepworth Studio, but there were also films from France and Norway – an indication of the international language of the silent film. At the Gaiety, as elsewhere during the war, serials like *The Broken Coin*, *Secret of the Submarine* and *Patria* were very popular. Serials were a staple attraction of the popular cinema from the First World War until the 1940s. Cheaply made, they were shown in successive weekly parts, each concluding with a 'cliff-hanger' ending.

While many early picture halls were conversions from churches, the Gem, on Elswick Road at its junction with Park Road, was originally a private school belonging to James Marchbanks.

In February 1909 Joseph Dobson planned to open the large schoolroom as a billiard hall, but the city council refused a licence. In June of the next year plans were approved for a picture hall. Unusually, the screen was to be mounted on a long wall, with the seats radiating around it. The cinema was to seat 190 in the stalls (the floor of the room) and 229 in the 'circle' (a stepped platform at the rear). In February a bioscope room was added. After initial refusal of a licence because of insufficient fire appliances, this was granted on 8 March 1911. The proprietors were the Northumberland Animated Picture Company and the manager a well-known local musician, Percy Forde.

When the Gem opened on 6 April 1911, seating had been reduced from 419 to 350. There were shows twice nightly and a Saturday matinée. The projector was a Tyler Triumph and a 'very fine baby grand pianoforte is presided over most ably by Miss Agnes Harvey.' The Gem does not seem to have been a great success, despite Miss Harvey's efforts, the licensee

changing twice in 1911. On 1 November the cinema was taken over by George Tully Tomkins and it was presumably then that its name was changed to Rendezvous. As the cinema never advertised in the press, it can only be assumed that it closed some time in 1912.

In November 1909, a local newspaper reported: 'We understand that a large house near to Heaton Station, and known locally as "Temple's Folly", has been purchased by a syndicate, and is to be adapted to the purposes of assembly and recreation rooms.' This building is presumably what became the Heaton Electric Palace in North View which, along with a billiard hall and a ballroom (this last opened early in 1911 as a roller-skating rink, the 'Palace Rink'), was owned by the Heaton Assembly Hall Company. The whole set-up was very similar to the almost contemporary Brighton complex at the opposite side of the city and was said to have cost about £30,000. The cinema, opened probably on 21 November 1910, was on the stadium plan and seated 925. The circle and stalls seats were plush tip-ups; the pit seats leather-covered tip-ups. There were also boxes, seating seven, at 5s.

The Electric Palace showed the usual suburban fare of comedies and serials, with 'refined and high-class' variety. The latter could be unusual: in April 1914 Martin Breedis, 'the great Russian athlete', wrestled all comers, Graeco-Roman style. The 'Favourite Resort of Heatonians' soon abandoned variety to concentrate on films alone. There were two changes of programme weekly with seat prices relatively high at 4d to 1s 3d. There was an unusually large orchestra of eight under W.G. Foggin. A café had been added by 1921.

After this rush to build – 19 picture halls opened between

December 1909 and November 1911 – the frenzied pace slowed noticeably with only two suburban halls opened in the next four years. All the picture halls detailed in this and the previous chapter were unashamedly intended for the 'working classes'. They were referred to in the cinema trade as 'industrial', a word which neatly described both their location and their audiences. Despite their owners' pretensions, with much use in cinema names of 'Grand' and 'Palace', they were very basic. Picture halls were a new form of enterprise, with many owners feeling their way: some failed, but most were successful.

Heaton Electric Palace, North View, 1912.

The national cinema trade magazine, *Kinematograph and Lantern Weekly*, gave a snapshot of the Newcastle picture hall scene at the end of 1910. 'From a small and lowly position, in the short space of a year, the "picture show" has become the premier and most popular amusement. The artistic character of the films now shown, their adaptability to all phases of life and emotion, and the cheapness and comfort of the many shows, explain their success'. The article claimed that a steady influx of 'all classes of patrons' had occurred and that the family party was now much more in evidence. Films of the funeral of Edward VII had 'done more than anything else to raise the status of the business. Many patrons were visibly affected, while many came who had never before entered a picture theatre'.

At times, the 'industrial' hall must have been bedlam, with children running about, constant chattering and shouting and the eating of fish and chips. *Northern Lights*, in an article in January 1920, gave a series of rather cruel descriptions of 'typical' picture theatre patrons, among whom was:

> … the lady with an awful yell, who will scream out just at the most exciting part of the picture, 'Hit 'em, knock 'em doon, eh, man, look at that now. Well yer, well I divvent knaw. Would yer believe?' Somebody behind shouts out, 'Shut up, wummon', and the lady gets on her dignity and off her seat, and expresses her opinion of the person who had the audacity to tell her to shut up. 'We wast telled me to shut up? 'Twas ye, ye greet big lump o' nowt, if I wasn't howding this ere bairn aad come acrost there and knock lumps off ye, mind ah wad an' all. What d'ye call yersel, anyhow, yer greet big bubbly beast, eh? Here's a penny, gan and get yersel run ower …

Some cinemas used lecturers to explain the pictures and to point up moral lessons: Lindon Travers was an early exponent of this art. F.W. Morrison, chairman of the Northern Branch of the Cinematograph Exhibitors' Association, explained in August 1926 that '…the lecturing was a farce and was soon dispensed with. There was an idea that people could not understand the picture.' Despite this, lecturer T.V. Padden was still advertising his services in 1920. Morrison was defending the north east against a charge made by film financier C.M. Woolf that cinemas employed people to read titles aloud, as some of the audience could not read while others could not read quickly enough. Despite Morrison's rebuttal of this 'libel', both Edward Davison, writing about the Raby and Agnes Smurthwaite on the Minerva mention that members of the audience were constantly asking their neighbours to read titles for them. This is confirmed by the *Northern Lights* article part-quoted above.

From the earliest days, cinema owners and managers were firm adherents of the Proverb 'Train up a child in the way he should go: and when he is old, he will not depart from it.' Children were attracted into the cinemas by special shows at low prices, usually 1d. At some cinemas –

T. Vincent Padden advertises his services as a lecturer ('Remember, he not only explains Pictures, but ENTERTAINS') in Northern Lights, 2 March 1920.

the Sun is an example – admission could be gained on production of clean jam-jars; the rate of exchange was one 2lb or two 1lb jars for one penny. In addition to the films, matinées offered gifts, competitions and prizes.

The musicians struggled against all the noise. Initially, musical accompaniment to films was provided by a single pianist who attempted to match the action on the screen. Most cinema owners tried to gather sufficient musicians to dignify with the name 'orchestra', though this often meant a trio or a quartet. The orchestra brought its own problems: with little or no time for rehearsal, any improvement in sound quality was often nullified by the inability of the players to improvise effectively while remaining a musical unit. Despite this, according to the trade magazine report of December 1910, many picture halls, for example the Olympia and the Grand, had first-class orchestras, although some picture halls tried 'to do it on the cheap, with nerve-racking results'.

It is a curious fact that the great periods of cinema openings, 1908-10 and the early 1930s were also periods of high unemployment and poverty. It appears that the old cliché that picture halls provided an escape from the hard reality of life was always true. While some among early cinema audiences had transferred their allegiance from the music hall and the variety theatre, 'in the main the vast majority of picture house patrons were not in the habit of attending other places of entertainment. The cheapness of this form of amusement has created what is really a new type of audience…' The picture halls were small, intimate and above all local; there was now no need to travel to the city centre for a night out. For music hall patrons, the transfer of loyalty to films was eased by the inclusion of variety acts in the programmes of suburban cinemas. 'Turns' were said to be improving in quality by late 1910, although some managers still appeared to think that 'any old (or young) thing' good enough.

Suburban or 'industrial' halls were distinguished by their low seat prices and the fact that they opened in the evenings only, when their potential audience had finished work. They almost invariably had two separate 'houses' at 7 pm and 9 pm. The type of film shown also distinguished them: in the words of *Northern Lights*, 'heavy melodrama, knock about comedy or ultra sentimental dramas'. In the city centre, picture halls like the Royal moved over to continuous performances starting in early afternoon, where patrons could enter at any point in the programme. This catered for the more casual patron who was just passing and wished to spend an hour of two in the cinema.

By the end of this period, the films themselves had increased both in length and in sophistication of content. In the first decade of the century, picture hall proprietors had moved away gradually from a mixed programme of story films (features), 'interest' films (documentaries), topicals (newsreels) and comedies, to a greater preponderance of feature films, with the other items used as programme fillers. By the outbreak of the First World War, fairly long feature films were not uncommon, lasting five or more reels. (A reel held about 1,000 feet of film with a running time of approximately ten minutes. A five-reel film therefore ran for about 50 minutes, and so on.)

A rewinder, 1919.

4 Cinemas for the middle-classes 1912-1914

The cinema-going experience was rather different in the A-class houses in the city centre. These were the 'picture palaces' built by the serious money which came into the exhibiting side of the business after 1912. The intention of this new breed of cinema owner (most operating as limited companies) was to drive the business up-market, attracting what was known as the *ton patron* rather than the exclusively working-class audience which had hitherto been drawn to the cinema. Ladies, after a morning shopping in town, were invited to pop into a cinema to enjoy the film and relax in the 'dainty cafés' which most city centre venues offered. There was much emphasis on good taste, refinement and opulent decoration; features unknown to the 'industrial' halls.

As the *Evening Mail* put it in December 1913:

We enter the marble portals of a lustrous and palatial building, pass by a pillar of politeness in uniform and brass buttons, receive a perforated disc of metal in exchange for a coin of the realm, tread the steps of thickly carpeted stairs, sip a 'café noir' in a luxurious lounge, and adjourn to a dim region of dreamy music and softly diffused ruby lights.

Cinemas of this kind showed first-run films in good condition, accompanied by an orchestra of ten or more players.

They showed films only and did not mix in any variety acts or 'turns'. Uniformed doormen, page boys selling sweets and chocolates, and 'girl attendants' made cinema going an event. Patrons of these cinemas need not fear that they would have to share these facilities with hoi polloi, who were likely to be deterred by the superior setting and product on offer. Cinemas carried over from theatres the simple class divisions based on seat prices, which in these middle-class halls were usually in the range of 6d to 1s 6d. In addition, there was invariably a separate entrance and pay box (often down a side-alley) for patrons of the cheapest seats, a tradition which applied even in the cinemas built in the 1930s. Afternoon as well as evening performances were normal.

The first example of this type of cinema in Newcastle was the Picture House (occasionally known as the Cinematograph Picture House), owned by the Newcastle Cinematograph Company and costing a reported £4,500 to build. The land at the junction of Westgate Road and Clayton Street was part of the Cross House site, leased from the city council. The cinema was opened before the builders had finished:

It is not yet complete, there is still the tower to be built at the angle of Clayton Street and Westgate Road [this was never built] **and there is still an artistic scheme of mural and ceiling decoration to be carried out as soon as the**

Clayton Street, with The Picture House at right, c.1915.

plaster work is dry; but even in its present state visitors will be impressed by its handsome appearance. Except for the balcony at the Clayton Street end, there is nothing to break the four square walls of the building. The lights are all concealed within the cornice that runs round the four walls, and the one thing that attracts attention above all others is the screen, artistically enclosed as it is in a proscenium of Corinthian design. There is more than the usual rake in the floor, so that the occupants of the tip-up chairs can see without interruption every picture that is shown. [The hall was to be run] … as a picture show purely and simply and to keep the entertainment going continuously from 2 till 11pm. Thus patrons may enter or leave at any time, and visitors to Newcastle who have trains to catch may, by the assistance of the electrically lit clock near the stage, time their departure to a minute.

The Picture House opened 12 February 1912 with a charity performance for the benefit of the Home for Destitute Crippled Children at Gosforth. Trading must have been successful, as in February 1913 a further part of the Cross House site was leased from the city. The cinema was extended to the rear, increasing capacity to 1,021 and permitting the addition of a tea room and a smokers' lounge. The decor was made considerably more opulent. Teas were served in all parts. These alterations were complete by November 1913. In early 1914 the orchestra was said to be Viennese, led by the almost unpronounceable Herr Franz Csavojacz. Also in that year, the cinema's name was amended to Westgate Road Picture House as a result of the opening of the Newcastle Picture House in Grey Street.

Newcastle Chronicle & Journal Ltd.

The Picture House orchestra and staff, c.1914.

The second luxurious picture theatre opened in the city centre was the Empire Cinema, converted from the shop premises of Dunn and Dick, jewellers. It was built by Moss Empires, who owned the adjacent Empire Theatre in Newgate Street. It was an unusual example of theatre proprietors building a cinema which was intended to operate as a unit with the original theatre.

The entrance was on Grainger Street West and up to first floor level had pillars of Hoptonwood stone, between which were mahogany doors and fittings. The foyer, with payboxes in the centre, was laid with marble slabs on floor and walls. 'Sumptuous' tea rooms (run by Tilley's) were provided and access was made from all parts of the building to the Empire Theatre, 'so that patrons wishing to spend an hour in the cinema, and then have a part of the evening in the theatre, can pass from one to the other without coming into the street, and special tickets will be issued and special facilities provided to enable them to do so.'

The auditorium, 68 by 42 feet, held 614; the circle was unusual in that it had a wide slip running along one wall towards the proscenium. Tip-up chairs in rose-pink were used throughout. The decoration was in the Adam style; the walls up to seven feet panelled in mahogany with cedarwood carvings. Above this were friezes and tapestries. The 16 by 14 foot screen was set in a fibrous plaster proscenium arch; projection was from the rear of the stalls. The auditorium lighting was indirect, projected from the electric lamps on to the ceiling from which it was reflected, 'a system which gives a most pleasing effect and avoids strain on the eyes'. Much was made of the Ozonair ventilation system, which was said to remove all stuffiness from the atmosphere, dissolve smoke and dissipate any fog which might get into the building.

On the first floor was a large tea room with a separate entrance from Grainger Street and access from the Empire Theatre. It was decorated in the Treillage style – ' a decoration much in vogue in London, but which has not yet been introduced in the North of England'. There was also a smokers' lounge and a further tea room on the second floor.

The Empire opened on Wednesday, 2 April 1913 at 6 pm: after opening night, performances were continuous 2 - 10 pm. Incidental music was by the New Empire Cinema Orchestra, supplemented by an organ. The cinema's modest little press advertisements during its early years – 'An excellent programme, with charming music' – contrast sharply with the more aggressive approach of the nearby Grainger to

Tony Moss

The Empire, Grainger Street West, 1930.

the marketing of its product. It is not known whether the proposed transfer tickets to the Empire Theatre were ever used, but if they were, the constant tramping to and fro must have been an irritation to the patrons of both places.

Since 1909 there had been several attempts to develop a site off Northumberland Street, between Northumberland Place and Lisle Street as a large concert venue, but all had failed. Finally in 1913 the Queen's Hall was built. The cinema was opened privately by the Lord Mayor on 8 September 1913, with the public opening the next day; there was a programme of Zenith films of Lily Langtry, Seymour Hicks and Ellaline Terriss in their stage successes, the beginning of a tradition of superior programming at the Queen's Hall.

The Empire auditorium, 1926.

Fare of this high quality will be seen under exceptionally comfortable circumstances … From all seats, owing to the semi-circular formation, and the sloping floor, all will get an uninterrupted view, and from an armchair upholstered in red plush. The whole hall, which seats 1,200, is carpeted in red, [which contrasts with] the grand circle ornamentations in white fibrous plaster. [Armchairs in inlaid rosewood and red plush were specially designed for the grand circle and the private boxes on each side of the hall at circle level.] … Not only is comfort assured by the seats, the wide gangways, the lounge entrances, and the elaborately fitted retiring rooms; but, if the place was filled with black smoke, it could be freed and sweet again in 12 minutes [this seems a long time] so complete is the ventilation system. The panelling is of oak, and the plen-

tiful introduction of natural foliage, lend a delightfully furnished aspect to the whole.

The plain elevation to the narrow Northumberland Place gave no hint of the opulence within; it quite justified its claim to be 'Newcastle's Finest Picture Theatre.' Musical accompaniment was by H.G. Amers' Bijou Orchestra. Access to the circle and 'first stalls' was from Northumberland Street; to the stalls from Northumberland Place and to the orchestra stalls from Lisle Street.

According to *Northern Lights*, much of the Queen's Hall's early success was due to its manager Fred Wolters who came to Newcastle late in 1913 and 'took control of … a young and puling business, and promptly changed what looked like

Front elevation of the Queen's, 1970.

being a ghastly failure into an enormous success.' In March 1920 the Queen's was bought by Black's of Sunderland; an organ was installed in 1920 and throughout the twenties there was a large orchestra of 12-14 players. The Queen's was much used by renters for trade shows and previews; they insisted on the best. On occasion, films came with specially composed scores, such as *The Sea Beast* (John Barrymore) and the French *Les Miserables*. George Black was keen on live prologues to films: *The Sea Beast* had such a prologue in

which the Lyric Quartette sang sea shanties, while showings of *Volga Boatmen* were preceded by a local male voice choir who hauled a rope across the narrow stage, all the while singing the title music – in Russian!

At the north end of Grainger Street was the Grainger Picture House, opened on 1 December 1913. It was built by a £10,000 company controlled by Joseph R. Collins, already a cinema owner, and S. Bamford, a stained glass manufacturer, and was a conversion from the business premises of Millings the drapers. It had shops on either side and offices above; the narrow entrance led to an auditorium parallel to the street.

This entrance, described in 1913 as 'imposing', was flanked by granite columns and gave on to a marble-lined vestibule. The stairs and passages were of marble with mahogany panelling. Stairs led to the circle and also to a café, which in addition had independent access from the street. The general style was very similar to the near-contemporary Empire. The auditorium was in the neo-Classical style, the ceiling pierced by three domes; the walls featured massive columns and modelled figures. The proscenium arch was flanked by four columns and surmounted by 'a magnificent group of sculpture'. The colour scheme – 'the essence of good taste and refinement' – was designed to be restful. The Grainger was probably unique among Newcastle's cinemas in that it was claimed that all contractors were city-based: even the seats were by the Patent Automatic Seat and Engineering Co. of St James' Street.

The Grainger achieved an initial coup, opening with the Edison Kinetophone, one of the early sound-on-disc systems:

The method by which the results are achieved is simple in explanation only. An attachment by wire operates a gramophone behind the screen at the same moment as the picture is released, and the projected photographs become, to all intents and purposes, live persons. They sing, perform on musical instruments, act plays, and do various other things, and if one is not self-deceived, he is at least wonderfully impressed with the absolute realism of the thing.

The Grainger Picture House, 1928.

In fact, sound-on-disc systems were far from new, even in 1913, and the Edison system was far from perfect; there had been problems at the press show and the examples of sound films shown were very short. There were six altogether, complementing the normal programme of silent films.

After the excitement of its opening, the Grainger settled down to become a fairly routine cinema: the Wedgwood Café was much advertised, as was the orchestra conducted by Robert Smith. During the war, the Grainger management began eye-catching press advertisements, unafraid of the topical pun: 'Munitions of amusement for the working millions of patriots during the few hours of rest and recreation. NO FUNERALS are ever shown at the Grainger'. By 1916 the cinema's adverts were taking a whole column on the front page of the *Evening Chronicle*, which must have been expensive for a 775-seater, and the enthusiastic manager seems to have been reined in.

Provincial Cinematograph Theatres (PCT) was one of the first and largest national cinema circuits, established in 1909. Its policy was to build imposing cinemas in major centres of population: the company initially wanted a site in Northumberland Street in August 1910 and in March 1911 were reported to be negotiating for the Victoria Billiard Saloon at 10-12 Grey Street, a former music hall. But it was not until 1914 that the latter site was secured.

The frontage was altered relatively little and the cinema blended reasonably well into the splendid Grey Street. It was PCT custom to name their cinemas simply 'The Picture House', but as there was already a cinema of that name in the city, it opened as the Newcastle Picture House. When the cinema closed, a local newspaper referred to it as Tyneside's

first super-cinema, 'the leading picture house of the district at a time when all the others were run on very modest lines'. PCT's cinemas were deliberately designed and operated to appeal to middle- and upper-class patrons – the 'carriage trade', whose custom had so far eluded the business.

This philosophy is well expressed in the booklet produced for the opening of the cinema, in which the attempt to create the atmosphere of an exclusive club is very evident. This was picked up by the press:

The vestibule from Grey Street is decorated in rich marbles with an original design of leaded glass comprising the arms of the city and counties of Northumberland and Durham. The entrance hall and Foyer are of striking

beauty, carried out in white and grey marble with panels of delicate Breche rose marble ... There is an electric passenger lift for balcony patrons. On the right is the cloak room and telephone call office ... On the first and second floors are spacious Foyers panelled in oak and hung with tapestry and [they] are furnished with comfortable lounges where patrons may rest and meet their friends ... Leading from the Entrance Foyer is a cosy tea lounge, where refreshments are served, and where patrons may read papers and magazines ... Leading from the First Floor Foyer is a handsome smoke room and café in the late 17th century style. Situated on the balcony level and reached by the main staircase or lift is a large Wedgwood café ... For the convenience of patrons who are shopping, parcels may be addressed to the theatre to await their arrival or departure ...

For its importance, the Newcastle Picture House had a rather modest capacity of 927. It was opened on 6 May 1914 by Sir Francis Blake, who, in his speech, outlined one of the arguments made by those who advocated cinemas as likely to save the people from a much greater evil: drink.

The coming of the picture house was one of the most notable features in modern life. The popularity of the cinematograph was a sign of the change in the condition of the people, of their ... determination to use some of the increased leisure which they enjoyed ... in harmless amusement and pleasure.

The Grey Street Picture House, 1922. The original name can be seen above the windows.

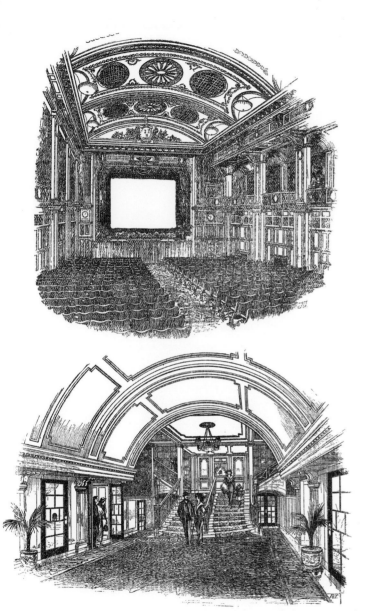

Top, the screen and below, the splendid foyer of the Newcastle Picture House.

Picture House Cafes

⁋ *A combination of rest, recreation, and a table of good things in fresh, wholesome and delicious variety.*

GOOD taste and harmony are worked into Picture House Cafes and ease is atmospheric. The prevailing notes are character, refinement, cosiness and elegant simplicity—that type of simplicity which is the essence of true excellence. The Cafes are open to the public whether visitors to the Picture Theatre or not.

There were two cafés at the Picture House – the Wedgwood Café, and the Smoke Lounge and Oak Room.

5 Four theatre conversions 1917-1930

In the years leading up to the First World War, it became increasingly evident that traditional theatres and music halls were failing to compete with picture halls for audiences. The cheapness of most picture halls was a real challenge and some theatres had begun to intersperse films with their stage acts. One of these was the Grand Theatre in Wilfred Street, off Shields Road, Byker. A large 1,820-seat venue opened in 1896, the Grand had had the occasional bioscope performance since Downey's Living Pictures had appeared in 1899, returning in 1907 as part of a Sunday series of sacred concerts with Lindon Travers. In December 1908 *The Bioscope* reported that 'pictures were thrown on the screen before the usual show commences' and in 1909 there was a 'picture season' ending in August. Variety and pictures seem to have become a feature by 1910, when the Grand took out a cinematograph licence, but there was no permanently constructed operating box until 1913, when part of the gallery was so used.

In 1913 the Grand was taken over by George Black who continued the pictures and

The Grand Theatre, Wilfred Street, Byker, c.1910.

variety seasons. During the war, many of the pictures were accompanied by the lecturer J.C. Padden (cousin of T.V. Padden see page 42); Friday night was given over to a full variety programme. By 1915 variety only was featured, but films and variety were back by 1917. In 1920 the Grand became part of the Thompson and Collins circuit, but the cine-variety policy continued until 1928, when the theatre was bought by Gaumont-British; variety acts tailed off to one each show.

The Pavilion Theatre in Westgate Road had also included the bioscope as part of its programme since opening in 1903. It occasionally had special film performances like the Kinemacolour *Eruption of Mount Etna* in 1911, and it was in financial trouble by 1913. At a shareholders' meeting on 10 March the chairman, Councillor E.J. Wilkinson stated that: '… the company was at present in a critical position, and this had been brought about by certain financial charges they had to meet, heavy artists' salaries, and competition they had to encounter, there being in the city centre now a great many picture halls. There were no less than 24 or 26 picture halls, three theatres, and four music halls.'

£10,000 was needed to clear the company of debt and the whole theatre was in need of decoration. A suggestion that the theatre should be converted into a picture hall was rejected after a long discussion. A committee was formed to seek a solution but without success, the Pavilion closing on 24

The Pavilion, Westgate Road, as a variety theatre, c.1916.

March 1913. A new company – the City Varieties Co. – with which George Black was involved, took over the Pavilion and reopened it in November with a programme of pictures and varieties – 'a concession to the taste of the moment.' The management clearly believed that – despite all the evidence – moving pictures were a passing fad and that variety would again be supreme. By late 1914 pictures were firmly at the bottom of the bill and in 1915 were abandoned altogether. But the variety and other programmes at the Pavilion were second-rate: a succession of tatty revues and musical farces and it closed on 30 June 1917.

When it reopened on 10 December 1917 it was as the New Pavilion, firmly devoted to films and under new management, the Scala (Newcastle) Ltd. Due to the war little alteration was made to the building, although much was promised for the future. The opening was low-key and without ceremony.

The operating box was backstage, using rear projection. Seating capacity was just over 1,600 which included, in theatre style, 134 standing and a gallery which could – at a push! – hold 600. The managing director was John Graham Cutts who left the New Pavilion in 1920 to become one of Britain's best known film directors between the wars.

The first film shown was D.W. Griffith's 178-minute epic *Intolerance*, which ran until 5 January 1918. This was an exceptional film which had opened in London at the Drury Lane Theatre. At the New Pavilion there were only two performances each day, at 2.30 pm and 7 pm and a 'symphony orchestra' was assembled to accompany the film. This orchestra of 40 players – unusually large for a cinema – was retained after *Intolerance* came off and gave promenade con-

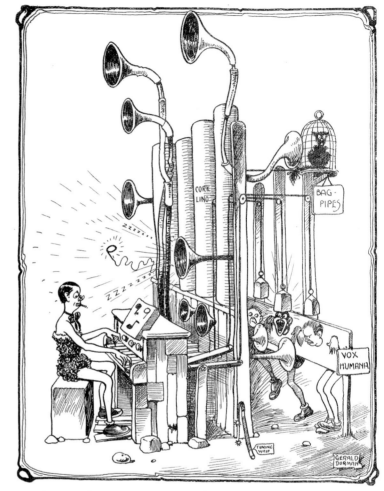

Northern Lights satirises 'Ye Grande Pipe Awgan' in 1920.

certs to afternoon audiences. Moving over to continuous (2 pm - 10 pm) performances, the cinema continued to attract first-run films, accompanied by topicals and Pathé News.

In September 1919 the promised improvements were completed. The stage was cut back and the space gained used to create a 'floral garden' which surrounded the orchestra. A large manual pipe organ costing £2,000 was installed. In the auditorium the pit was eliminated and replaced with tip-up chairs and the whole redecorated and recarpeted: '… charmingly garbed courteous attendants [were] on hand to lead the way to the seat you require…' All this was achieved without closing the cinema and of course had nothing to do with the opening of the almost adjacent Stoll a few months earlier.

Double features (of good quality) were now the rule and in October 1919 a fairly typical programme in 'The House of Music' offered two features, *Marriages are Made* (Peggy Hyland) and *Cecilia of the Pink Roses* (Marion Davies, 'the prettiest girl on the screen') and the Grand Orchestra playing selections from *Cavalliera Rusticana* with Francois Grandpierre ('England's Foremost Cinema Violinist') and Harry Davidson ('England's Greatest Cinema Organist'), the latter lured from the Stoll.

The Tyne Theatre, almost adjacent in Westgate Road, like the Pavilion, had been in difficulty in the years just before the First World War. Opened in 1867, it had for decades rivalled the Theatre Royal in the quality of its productions. By April 1913 the Tyne had been forced to accept moving pictures on occasion. A projection box of steel plates was constructed backstage: rear projection meant that the auditorium was unaltered and could easily revert to theatrical use.

Throughout the war the main fare at the Tyne continued to be provincial tours of London stage suc-

British Film Institute

The Stoll, previously the Tyne Theatre, Westgate Road, c.1925.

cesses, visits by travelling opera companies and of course the annual pantomime. In mid-1916 it was home to an extended run of D.W. Griffith's 192-minute epic *Birth of a Nation*: it was quite usual at this period for theatres to take the premier runs of major films, much to the annoyance of cinema owners. Cecil B. De Mille's *Joan the Woman*, starring the American opera singer Geraldine Farrar, was shown at the Theatre Royal in July 1918, the only occasion on which this theatre is known to have shown a film. Such prestige shows certainly attracted an audience which would never go near an ordinary cinema.

On 1 March 1919 the Tyne Theatre closed and Sir Oswald Stoll acquired the lease, announcing on 12 April that he intended 'giving Newcastle the very best... The screen play will form the main feature of the entertainment, with all the instrumental, vocal, and colour effects which have made the Stoll Picture Theatre, London – formerly the London Opera House – so extremely attractive.' Stoll employed the noted theatre architect Frank Matcham to effect the transformation. To the subsequent gratification of theatre historians, his alterations were largely cosmetic: all the elaborate Victorian stage machinery was left intact.

The Stoll was officially opened on 2 June 1919 by the Lord Mayor, who purchased the first ticket from Sir Oswald's aged parent (she apparently performed this service at every theatre her son opened). The first film was an exclusive presentation of *Tarzan of the Apes* (Elmo Lincoln), supported by comedies and topicals. Shows were continuous 2 pm - 10 pm.

The press was intrigued by the fact that '[a] novelty in the matter of attendants is that at the dress-circle entrance are two young women attired in highwaymen's dress, this

Newcastle Weekly Chronicle for 3 June 1919 heralds the opening of the Stoll and its 'highwayman' attendants. The Lord Mayor buys the first ticket from Sir Oswald Stoll's mother.

style of costume having been adopted at all Sir Oswald Stoll's picture houses. The rest of the female attendants wear dresses of wine gabardine which harmonises with the tone of the whole place'.

The Stoll was a major cinema throughout the twenties, backed by Sir Oswald's control of a major London outlet – 'What the London Coliseum sees today, the Stoll, Newcastle, sees tomorrow.' The local management was also excellent:

W.H. Lindon Travers (son of Lindon Travers) was followed by Harry Samson. Travers introduced a patrons' weekly magazine, *The Stoll Sentinel* and *Tyne Tatler* (later *The Stoll Herald*) in February 1920, which continued until at least 1927, with details of current and future programmes and the stars appearing in them. Films were supported by the Stoll Symphony Orchestra, a Grand Organ, and variety acts. Always willing to experiment, in June 1922 the Stoll acquired a Vitasona sound effects machine.

The fourth conversion of a theatre to cinema use was John Grantham's Majestic Theatre on Condercum Road in Benwell, built conventionally with stalls, circle and boxes. The Majestic was opened by the Lord Mayor on 3 October 1927 with a performance of the comedy revue *Off the Dole*. In May 1928 it became the base for one of Alfred Denville's stock companies, with a series of 'West End comedy, American crook plays, and standard classic dramas.' The long Denville season ended in April 1930; a few weeks later the Majestic appears to have closed as a theatre, reopening as a cinema on 4 August 1930 with the

talkie *Men without Women.*

A fifth Newcastle theatre could have shown films had the need arisen: this was the Hippodrome, Northumberland Road, opening on 23 November 1912. This vast building, formerly the White City, a skating rink and dance hall, had a cinematograph licence until closure on 20 May 1933, but films appear never to have been shown there.

Tony Moss

The Majestic, Condercum Road, c.1937.

6 The Twenties – the Talkies 1919-1930

Only a handful of new cinemas opened in the city in the twenties: as early as December 1919 the *Newcastle Daily Chronicle* reported that the wartime cinema boom had ended, which it believed was accounted for by the longer opening of public houses, 'the tightening of money, and the fact that people, and especially the women folk, no longer have need to seek relief from anguishing thoughts occasioned by the war.' There was also, just after the war, a shortage of building materials, so that even those who wished to venture into cinema ownership found it all but impossible.

So, although there were some attempts to build cinemas in various parts of the city in the year immediately after the war, only one was successful. The Jesmond, the first cinema in a large middle-class residential area, was financed by a limited company formed in December 1919 with a capital of £20,000. Hugh Smith, a wine and spirit merchant, was chairman. The company bought a site immediately opposite West Jesmond Station and although the foundations were laid in December 1919, it was not until May 1921 that the cinema opened.

Notable features of the cinema were the reverse rake of the floor in the front stalls (or pit), 'thus enabling the occupants of those seats to look at the pictures without the usual backward craning of the neck', and a concave screen which was said to give an undistorted picture from any angle. The

Newcastle artist, Gerald Dorman, was responsible for the scenic effects in the auditorium. The total cost of land and building was £34,775, an indication of the inflationary effect of the war: a prewar cinema of similar size, the Scala, Heaton, had cost £7,000.

The Jesmond, 'a cosy and comfortable house', was opened by the vice-chairman of the board, Errington Dunford on 2 May 1921, who assured the audience that it was absolutely fireproof and that it had 'the largest cubic space per person of any place of entertainment in the city.'

The Jesmond opens its doors, Weekly Chronicle, 2 May 1921.

At the opening, which was a matinée, local residents were the guests of the management and saw, as the main feature, *At the Mercy of Tiberius*. The first manager was John Fenwick, late of the Heaton Electric Palace.

Despite the management's grand gesture on opening day, the cinema was not a success. Was Jesmond not a suitable area for a cinema? In 1921 it was still considered very much a working-class venue. Was the management or the programming at fault? Whatever the reason, the Jesmond closed in late January 1922. The owning company went into liquidation and the building was offered for sale on 18 September 1922.

It was bought for £20,000 by H.P. Smith, one of the directors of the original company and sold on at the same figure to a newly formed company, the Jesmond Picture House Co. (1922) Ltd. The directors of the latter were virtually the same as for the original company but with the addition of the experienced James MacHarg. The Jesmond was redecorated in brown and gold and reopened in the week of 4 December 1922.

The Scotswood Cinema was one of the smallest in the city. It was a conversion to cinema use of the former St Margaret's Mission Church, a corrugated iron building below and to the east of the railway embankment leading to

St Margaret's Mission Church, Scotswood, 1900, which became the Scotswood Cinema.

Scotswood Bridge. The interior was 62 feet long and only 24 feet wide, with a small stage at one end. The walls were of varnished pitch pine, a potentially appalling fire hazard; possibly because of this, although the cinema was designed for 324 seats, all on the level floor, it was licensed for only 290, with no standing permitted. The owner was John Richard Scott, who had formed the Scotswood Cinema Co. Ltd., in February 1926, with £500 in £1 shares; his partner was Thomas Charlton, late of the Picture Theatre, Lemington.

The Plaza, May 1935.

The Scotswood probably opened in April 1926.

Nothing is known of the programmes at this cinema, which never advertised in the press. It is one of the few cinemas in the city to which entrance could be gained on the presentation of clean jam-jars (which were sold on to a jam factory along Scotswood Road).

The Plaza in Fenham was built to complement a housing estate. The builders, H.T. and W.A. Smelt, had had cinema interests outside the city since 1912. In the twenties, the firm built much of the Milvain Estate and the cinema was a finishing touch. The cinema was at the junction of Westgate Road and Gowland Avenue. There was an 18-foot deep stage with a music room and six dressing rooms beneath. Space was provided for an orchestra and an organ. From the corner entrance the stalls lounge led off to the right and the pit lounge to the left; there was also a circle lounge. Two small shops were included in the frontage to Westgate Road.

The Plaza was officially opened on 6 February 1928 by the Sheriff of Newcastle. The opening film was *McFadden's Flats* (Chester Conklin) with an organ recital by Herby Laws of the Coliseum, Whitley Bay and a musical interlude by the Morlais Quartette. The proceeds of the opening performance were donated to the Royal Victoria Infirmary. Performances were continuous from 6 pm. Films arrived at the Plaza about eight weeks after their city centre showing and initially were of the best. The stage facilities were used for 'variety diversions' every Friday.

The Welbeck Cinema and Playhouse at the corner of Scrogg Road and Byker Street, Walker, was the last cinema of the silent era to be opened in the city. It was built by a company formed in December 1928, with a capital of £14,000 in £1 shares, whose chairman was William Crocker, a Wallsend fruit merchant. There was a large 30 feet deep stage,

with dressing rooms below and an orchestra pit. The auditorium seated 965, and was 'Comfortably warm in winter and cool in summer, the auditorium is at all times well ventilated and absolutely clean in every way.' A lounge was available for circle patrons and there was a free car park.

The cinema was opened by the Lord Mayor-elect on 4 November 1929. The first performance was by invitation and

The Welbeck, 1967.

programmes in the first few weeks were not advertised. There were twice nightly shows; seats could be booked. From 16 December 1929 there was a 'grand variety week' with a singer, a comedian and a trapeze act, in addition to the films. But stage acts, despite 'Playhouse' in the cinema's name, were infrequent. Even before the Welbeck opened four of the six dressing rooms were converted for storage. However 'turns' appeared occasionally up to the war.

The Westgate Road Picture House now faced competition from the Pavilion and the Stoll, a hundred yards away, and in about 1919 was taken into the Consolidated Cinematograph Theatres circuit. The new owners added a 'splendid marble entrance' in February 1920. CCT leased yet more land in January 1922, presumably with the intention of enlarging the cinema again, but it was not until 1927 that a decision was taken to rebuild entirely. The Westgate closed on 5 March 1927.

The rebuilt cinema opened as the New Westgate on 31 October 1927, with its capacity greatly increased to 1,870, and decorated in the Italian Renaissance style. It was for a few years the city's largest cinema. There is a persistent story that the new cinema was designed without a projection box, which had to be added at the last minute. This seems barely credible, but would account for the box being on the roof, with a very steep 27 degree rake to the screen.

Existing suburban picture halls continued on their unremarkable way through the twenties. The Adelaide was sold by W.H. Rewcastle to the Faith family in 1919. It was possibly when Charles Faith took over that a shallow, two-storey stone-faced annex was built to the right of the hall, forming a foyer with offices above. Faith reportedly sold

Top, the New Westgate, 1927. Below, the auditorium.

the Adelaide to two London cinema owners, L.J. Clements and N.D. Fitzgerald, for about £10,000 in April 1928; under this management this small picture hall was one of the nuclei of the Union Cinemas circuit and must have surprised the trade by becoming the third city cinema to install sound.

The general manager of the Brighton complex was James Coverdale Bell who stayed at the cinema until his retirement in 1946. A founder of the local branch of the Cinematograph Exhibitors' Association, he was a close friend of London-based Geordie Sidney Bacon and the latter's booking manager, Thomas France. The Brighton's films were booked by France until 1935; during the First World War they were identical to those shown at the Olympia in the city centre and a cut above the fare at the normal suburban cinema.

Bell had grand plans for the development of the Brighton which he revealed to *Northern Lights* in December 1919: 'When completed the cinema will seat approximately 1,800, the dancing room will accommodate 400 on the floor and the billiard saloons will be equipped with 29 tables. This scheme will necessitate extensive structural alterations, and with the other internal improvements foreshadowed will, Mr. Bell says, involve a sum of no less than £100,000'. This investment seems to have been too much for Newcastle Entertainments Ltd. to contemplate and the alterations were never made. The Sidney Bacon connection enabled the Brighton to stay in the front rank of suburban cinemas.

Edward Davison, who ran the Raby (often imposingly known as the Raby Grand) in Byker as a bingo hall from 1961, contributed his rather humorous memories of the cinema to the *Byker Phoenix* in 1980:

The whole of the downstairs was fitted out with long wooden forms. You were told to shove up a bit and were eventually squeezed out and finished up on the floor ... The orchestra consisted of Johnny Carse on the piano, his wife, whom he met at the Raby, played violin, and Mr. Mitchell, who worked during the day at W.H. Holmes Paintworks as a cooper, played bass fiddle ... Variety acts were introduced between films. They were very good and worked hard for their coppers. I remember the busty sopranos, tenors, ventriloquists and in particular a gentleman who played 'The Bluebells of Scotland' on ropes of bells suspended from the flies. He was a riot. Magicians on the stage didn't stand a chance. The Byker lads would tell him how the trick was done, and during his performance would whistle and shout. 'Turn round, it's on your back'- 'It's under your dickie' – and

The Raby as a bingo hall, 1970.

'Hadaway and gerroff'.

Pathé's Gazette, usually about six weeks out of date, was rushed to the 'Bamburgh' for a double showing – then back to the Raby. Although Mick [Patton] pedalled like hell he was usually late. When he arrived the patrons were stamping their feet and shouting abuse at the manager.

A big event at the Raby was the Great Road Race, which was filmed by a newsreel cameraman friend. Hundreds of people packed Commercial Road to see the race and be filmed. You were invited to come to the Raby and see yourself on the screen … the best business the Raby ever did during the Silent Era was 'Alf's Button'. It was booked for three days and lasted the week. It was retained for a further week. The hall was packed twice nightly – the queues reaching as far as the Middle Club.

In Walker, the lease of the Mechanics' Institute was transferred to John Scott in 1913; he stayed for ten years. There were then continuous performances and a split week. Scott was succeeded by Baker and Roche, who already ran the Vaudeville nearby and who built a new proscenium in September 1923. The cinema was now a valuable asset to the committee of the Mechanics' Institute: hire of the hall accounted for £278 of the £564 income for 1924. There is some doubt as to whether the hall was open on a permanent basis in the late twenties: the trade magazine *Cinema* of 4 April 1928 says that it had been 'closed for a number of years'. Thomas B Roche did not take up the licence in January 1930: probably it was thought not worth while to go to the expense of installing

sound equipment and the Welbeck had recently opened as a rival.

The Scala, Heaton, had a rather more prosperous time of it. Throughout the twenties programmes at the Scala were superior, with 'First-class music by the Scala Orchestra'. From 1925 films were booked at the Queen's Hall by George Black; Scala audiences seeing the films which played at this first-run cinema after a ten week delay. In 1928 the national circuit General Theatres Corporation took over the Scala.

In August 1913 Benjamin Spoor took over the Sun at Long Row, Byker Hill, made a few minor alterations and ran it until closure in 1934. One anonymous correspondent to *Byker Phoenix* in 1980 recalled:

He was always immaculately dressed, a beautiful suit with his butterfly collar and bow tie, always a buttonhole of a carnation or rose and his button boots and spats! He always had in his hand a rolled up newspaper and would beat you over the head with it and shout 'Move along there, move along!' The seats in the cinema were only long wooden forms and we had to crouch together to make room for twice as many kids as it would hold … There was a little bit of a stage below the screen, on which there was a piano and a gentlemen called Mr Varley used to play this piano and watch the film at the same time. … He had the right tune for the action depicted and everybody got worked up into the spirit of things. He had various other gadgets at his side to give the effect of thunder, heavy rain, gun shots, storms, ghosts, etc. One thing that always sticks in my mind was a cowboy thriller, when Buck Jones (the fastest and toughest gun in the west – we thought!) lost his friend over a cliff. He landed badly hurt on a ledge and when our hero Buck found him, he tied his lariat to his horse and lowered himself over the cliff to his friend. He tied himself and friend together and called to his faithful horse to haul away and gee-up! The excitement was intense and silence reigned, but the poor horse couldn't make any progress, All of a sudden, in the intense silence and excitement, a voice from behind us shouted 'Gee up, ye wooden bugger!' Mr Varley started bashing on his piano and I think the horse must have heard as he suddenly started dragging the two unfortunates up the cliff.

The Sun occupied a warm place in many hearts: more recollections were given in a letter to the *Evening Chronicle* in August 1970: '[Entrance ticket numbers were flashed on the screen and] if your number came up your prize was 1lb of sausages or a packet of Tip Top peas. Both of my brothers won these prizes and my father sent me back to the next performance to try for the potatoes and believe it or not I won them and we had our dinner for the next day.' Bill Taylor and Ken Brown recalled independently that admittance to Saturday matinées could be gained for a couple of jam jars.

Admission prices declined throughout the twenties. There were two shows nightly and a

An advertisement from the Journal and North Star, 10 October 1926.

split week. Unlike most other cinemas, occasional variety shows were given right to the end. The Sun never installed sound and by 1934 must have been having difficulty in finding silent films to screen: it was last licensed on 2 February 1934 and closed later in the year.

In 1929, the Stoll was being readied for a new phenomenon – feature-length talking pictures. Developed in the United States to challenge the growing success of commercial radio, sound films revolutionised cinemas and cinema-going, although sound synchronised with film had been used for short subjects since the earliest days of film-making.

Con Docherty, who worked at the Queen's Hall, recalled one of the owner's initiatives:

… about 1927, this American, Lee de Forest, talked George Black into letting him come in with these original talkies lasting 10 to 15 minutes each in a sound on film system. These short sound films included a famous pianist of the day, Mark Hambourg, a famous tenor and an on screen accordion player who argued with a 'plant' in the audience:
Plant: I bet you couldn't play a request if I asked you to.
Accordionist: Who couldn't?
Plant: You couldn't.
Accordionist: Go on then, ask me.
Plant: Play 'Flight of the Bumble Bee'.'

These short revue items had been filmed at British Phonofilms' Clapham Studios, and preceded the first feature-length sound film shown in Newcastle by two-and-a-half years, being at the Queen's as support from 10 October 1926 until January 1927.

Lee de Forest's was a sound on film system; what the Stoll was preparing for was sound-on-disc. On 28 March 1929 the management announced that Western Electric was wiring the cinema for sound. It 'will be the first theatre in the city to present talking pictures as a principal feature in the programme. They will consist of dramas and comedies that will run for over an hour.' A new steel-framed screen was installed behind which were two giant loudspeakers, 14 feet high and slung from steel towers. The acoustical properties of this ex-theatre were said to be ideal for sound.

The Stoll's first talkie, *The Singing Fool* (Al Jolson) began a ten-week run on 11 May 1929. Hours were extended to 12.30 until 11pm. and stage shows were abandoned, along with the symphony orchestra. The impact of this first talkie was tremendous and was recalled sixty years later: Mrs Sewell remembered it 'with bated breath, although I was very very young at the time. The vast darkness and the 'black' face on the silver screen, plus the metallic sound. It was quite an awe-inspiring occasion.'

Les Irwin recalled: 'Talkies brought a vast difference. Prices went up for a start, our piano-player got sacked – a new kind of excitement prevailed. "Talkies – whatever next?" "They're just a passing fad" "Can't make out a word they say" were some remarks people made. Deaf people hated them. Large notices ordered patrons: SILENCE PLEASE and offenders who disobeyed, tipped up their seats noisily or otherwise offended were silenced by loud "Shhhs" and murderous looks.'

TALKING PICTURES

Newcastle Quite Mad Over Them.

QUEUES EVERYWHERE.

£7,000 Weekly Spent on Film Shows.

When Al Jolson sang "Sonny Boy" on the screen at the Stoll Picture Theatre last year, and kept Newcastle weeping for weeks, even those who wept with him in his sorrow vowed, between sobs, that the "talkies," like roller-skating, were but a phase of entertainment that would be short-lived.

Newcastle Journal, January 1930, describes the new phenomenon.

STOLL PICTURE THEATRE, NEWCASTLE-ON-TYNE.

12.30 p.m. to   Continuous   12.30 p.m. to
11 p.m.   11 p.m.
TO-DAY AND ALL THIS WEEK
THE TALKING PICTURE SUCCESS,
Al Jolson in " THE SINGING FOOL "
(Warner Bros. Vitaphone).
Approx. Times of Screening:
                12.45, 2.50, 4.50, 7.0, 9.0.
No Advance Booking.

7 The super-cinemas 1931-1938

At first, it was by no means certain that talkies would be a success. For many cinemagoers, the sound film was not an advance on the silent picture, which had evolved its own international language. The American accents of the early sound films were disliked by many and incomprehensible to some, although this was soon to change. In March 1930 the Stoll advertised *Under the Greenwood Tree* as a 'British 'Talkie' with British Voices', and as late as September that year the Brighton similarly promoted *The Bishop Murder Case* with 'Basil Rathbone, The Star who speaks good English'.

Two cinemas, the Grey Street and the Jesmond, proclaimed their loyalty to the silents. Small cinemas found the cost of adapting for sound a heavy burden and two, the Stanhope Grand and the Sun, closed. The best American sound-on-film systems by Western Electric could cost around £2,800, depending on the size of the cinema, with an annual maintenance charge of £280. There was also confusion over sound systems. Initially, only Western Electric equipment could play both sound-on-film and sound-on-disc: those cinemas with other systems eventually had to convert to sound on film. A film break with a sound-on-disc system was a disaster, as only the most skillful, or lucky, projectionists could successfully re-synchronise the two elements. At the Queen's Hall, projectionists were paid a bonus if they got through a week without a film break.

Such doubts as there were did not last: once they had got the hang of talkies, the cinema-going public loved them. Such

Mrs W. Huggins

Operating staff at the Queen's, 1932. Left, Ernest Brown, chief operator; below the projector is the sound-on-disc player.

was their popularity that the Queen's Hall's manager claimed in January 1930: 'We are doing phenomenal business and this week we are having four "capacity" houses a day. With silent films of the most popular type the average was two-and-a-half "capacity houses" in four performances. So great is the demand that on Saturday we are going to give a morning performance commencing at 10.15. I have known nothing like it.'

The coming of sound transformed cinema-going habits. Visits to the cinema became almost an obsession for much of the population. A correspondent to the *Evening Chronicle* in 1970 remembered: 'Our programme was: Monday, Hippodrome Theatre, Tuesday, Brighton, Wednesday, Plaza; then when the programme changed … Thursday, Brighton and on Friday to the Plaza.' Cinema-going of this intensity was far from uncommon. Many people had their 'own' cinema seats which they occupied with clockwork regularity whatever was showing. The more dedicated planned their outings with the help of magazines like *Picturegoer*.

It was not long before the industry began to respond to demand of this intensity. Its first expression in the city was by an American company, Famous-Lasky, later Paramount. Their plans for a 2,360-seat cinema in Pilgrim Street were approved by the city council in October 1929 and amended to a larger 2,602 seats in

Northumberland and Newcastle Society

The Paramount, Pilgrim Street, September 1931.

March 1930. Newcastle cinemagoers were stunned by the Paramount on its opening on 7 September 1931. Not only was it by far the largest seating capacity of any cinema yet built in the city, with opulent lounges and powder rooms, but the shows, with a first-class main feature, WurliTzer organ, large orchestra and Tiller Girls, were the nearest Newcastle came to the legendary American super-cinemas.

Paramount's policy was explained in a brochure produced for opening night:

The Paramount will screen exclusively the first presentation of the famous Paramount Pictures in the Newcastle area, as well as other productions of outstanding merit. With few exceptions there will be a complete change of programme each Monday. In addition to the full screen programme we will present each week original stage productions, musical and scenic novelties, the Paramount orchestra and the mighty WurliTzer organ. The stage presentations will be the famous Francis A. Mangan creations and will come direct from the Plaza Theatre, London. These stage spectacles are exclusively produced for the Paramount Theatres and cannot be seen elsewhere.

The opulence and splendour of the Paramount had to be seen to be believed. Bill Whitehead was present on opening night: 'The Paramount was the most beautiful theatre I have ever seen. It was known as "The Cathedral of Motion Pictures" [An epithet first used by the Roxy in New York]. One minute the theatre would be all in blue, then it was all in red, then green as the two colours were blended. When it

The Ladies' Powder Room at the Paramount.

Northumberland and Newcastle Society

opened it created a sensation because the usherettes were dressed in trousers of French grey; the reception ladies walked about with a tray with boxes of chocolates …'

Mrs Sewell recalled: 'One of the entrancing things about the Paramount was the Powder Room. It was very big and luxurious, lined with mirrors, [and] done out in pink and beige. It was absolutely the last word!' Even the Licensing Justices were impressed: they felt compelled to record in their minutes their satisfaction at the 'erection and equipment of the premises, which seemed to have embodied every possible comfort and convenience.'

The promises made in the policy statement were kept, for a time at least. Anton (late of the Opera House, Milan) was replaced by Vicoli as conductor of the symphony orchestra, which appeared under various guises, such as the Paramount Jazzmanians or the Syncopated Symphonic Orchestra, but all had gone by 1934. The Mangan Tiller Girls appeared less regularly after 1932 and were gone by 1933. Stage shows of other kinds were however retained until 1938: the best of these were the big-name British dance bands such as Billy Cotton, Jack Payne, Geraldo, Debroy Somers, Lew Stone, Jack Hylton, Roy Fox, Ambrose and Joe Loss. There were personal appearances by George Robey, Anna Neagle, Al Bowlly and George Formby. From its opening, the Paramount issued a weekly magazine for its patrons. There was said to be a staff of 200, including ten projectionists.

While they lasted, the stage features could be innovative: Cecil B. de Mille's *Cleopatra* was shown with a special prologue danced by Anton Dolin and Wendy Toye. The films themselves were not always of the best: there were many double-features and from time to time the stage acts were billed above the film. From May 1934 there were special reduced prices for the unemployed (as long as they got there before 1 pm) and in December 1936 the cinema began advertising '1,000 seats at 6d' up to 4 pm and evening prices were reduced to 1s to 2s 6d. This said, however, the Paramount was undoubtedly the city's premier cinema and a

The outer lobby at the Paramount, September 1931. Right, Cleopatra, 1934.

visit to it was a special event.

On 29 July 1939 the *North Mail* revealed that the provincial Paramounts were to be sold. The buyer was Oscar Deutsch's Odeon chain, which had been negotiating for some time. The change of owner-

72

ship took place on 27 November 1939; on 22 April 1940 the Paramount's name was changed to Odeon in its press advertising.

The arrival of the Paramount proved to be a catalyst for local cinema owners and signalled the beginning of a new burst of building. The first to appear was the Haymarket on the northern edge of the city centre. The company Haymarket Theatre (Newcastle) Ltd. was formed in June 1933, capitalised at £50,000. Its main promoter Dixon Scott (great great uncle of film directors Ridley and Tony Scott) had 25 years experience in the business; the profits from his small cinemas in Jarrow, Prudhoe and elsewhere enabled him to attract investors (many of whom had joined him in building the Prince's Theatre in North Shields in 1928).

Mr Bell [the architect] **has borne in mind the perfect comfort of its patrons in every respect. Although the building is large enough to seat 1,700 people, less than twelve hundred seats are installed. This sacrifice of seating accommodation has been made in order to give really ample space for each patron. Each floor has an adequate crush foyer … there is no need to climb any stairs to reach the Circle, for a lift is provided to enter it at two levels. The Circle seats have been chosen for luxury without regard to expense. They are throughout of the very**

Northumberland and Newcastle Society

The Paramount's royal circle, September 1931 – cinema-goers were stunned.

latest invention 'Dunlopillo', covered in velvet … The seats in the stalls are almost as luxurious as those in the Circle. They, too, are wonderfully spaced for comfort, there being three inches more between each row than is usual, even in the best of theatres … projection of the pictures should be perfect, for the good reason that the operating booth is placed below the Circle, instead of being placed high up at the back of the theatre, which is the common practice.

The Haymarket claimed to be the second cinema – after the Leicester Square Theatre – to be fitted with Western Electric 'wide-range' sound. The stage 'would be excellent for musical comedies and dramas not requiring a large cast, should it ever be needed for that purpose'. The Haymarket Café, above the entrance foyer, seated 150 and was leased to Hunter's the Bakers. 'The view from the Café windows – which extend right across an 80 feet frontage – is full of animation, as there is always something interesting happening in the Haymarket'.

Advertised as 'Newcastle's Luxury Theatre' the Haymarket was opened by comedian Tom Walls on 21 December 1933. After a programme of shorts and songs from the Prudhoe Gleemen, Walls' film *Just Smith* was shown. (This had played the Queen's the previous month). In the fashion of the time the Haymarket management stated its 'policy' for the future, rather modest for a major city centre cinema:

We shall not attempt to compete with the existing 'first-run' cinemas in the City, but shall show the most choice

ABC Haymarket, 1964.

pictures from all their programmes soon after their first exhibition. In this way, and in this way only, can any cinema be certain that its programme will never disappoint its patrons ... Our programmes will run for two-and-a-half hours continuously, and our short films will be chosen with as great care for their interest and entertainment value as the 'features'. We shall not pad out time with inferior 'fill-ups', 'interludes', or cheap trimmings, and we shall have NO MIGHTY ORGAN. Good pictures will occupy the whole time of our shows, which will, wherever possible, include two full-length 'features'. In our advertisements we shall avoid 'boosting' and 'stunting'.

RCHM

The Haymarket's vast auditorium in 1984. The extensions of 1936 can be seen in the circle.

Following this blatantly obvious attack on the Paramount, there was an appeal to local patriotism: 'The Haymarket theatre is the only modern cinema in the centre of Newcastle with independent management. All the other important cinemas are managed from London as units of big circuits.' There was also to be a 'special department' to make local newsreels – 'we hope in the process of time to gather together a notable local historical record in pictures.'- (if made, where are the newsreels now?).

From the outset, Haymarket programmes were of good quality, although they were chiefly second runs in the city. An early success was the all-star *David Copperfield* which ran for four weeks in late 1935, a Haymarket 'exclusive'. For some reason unknown, in November 1935 the Haymarket ceased to advertise in the local press and in May 1936 closed for rebuilding.

The alterations involved extending the cinema to the rear: the facade was untouched. Seating was increased from 1,200 to 2,002, although advertisements often claimed 2,200. The café was now run by Carrick's. The rebuilt Haymarket was opened by the Lord Mayor on 31 August 1936. At the opening ceremony, Dixon Scott announced that the cinema had been leased for 21 years to Associated British Cinemas Ltd. In fact, licensing records show a transfer from Dixon Scott to Arthur Moss (for ABC) on 6 September 1935, so it was ABC which made the decision to rebuild to gain a large first-run cinema in the city.

Under its new control the Haymarket had access to bigger pictures more quickly, especially the excellent Warner Brothers product of the late thirties and forties, but it was never advertised as aggressively as its size warranted. There were occasional band shows and a personal appearance by Charles Laughton on 3 August 1938.

The Apollo was the first of two super-cinemas to be opened on Shields Road, Byker, within a year. The site, formerly the Toll Bar House, had been selected by James MacHarg of Tyne Picture Houses Ltd. as early as 1920. The Apollo was officially opened by the Lord Mayor on Thursday 28 December 1933, all proceeds going to his Christmas Comforts Fund and the Byker Sun Ray Clinic.

'Get the Apollo habit' suggested early press advertisements: in one such, in February 1934, the cinema addressed its patrons: 'I, the Apollo, the Youngest Picture Theatre in the Newcastle area, hold over 1,600 people all comfortable and warm. I have heated waiting rooms for 1,000 people instead of queuing in the cold wet streets. My Western Electric Apparatus was acknowledged by everybody as the best in the district. It has been still further improved by adding Western Electric Wide Range, the latest sound invention. Note my prices … ' A free car park was opened at the side of the cinema, claiming to be the first in Newcastle, while in April 1935 an 18-table billiard hall was added.

Auditorium of the original Apollo, 1933.

Opening with evening shows only, in April 1934 the Apollo began to experiment with matinée performances, at first on Wednesday only but by 1937 every day. *Top Hat* (Astaire-Rogers) played four shows daily in February 1936 despite the fact that it had been shown at the Paramount only three weeks earlier.

Through the thirties, the Apollo was a considerable success. Morrison (Teddy) Fraser, manager from 1933, recalled for *Byker Phoenix*:

You must remember that they were the bad years, unemployment was rife, people hadn't very much money, and things were tough. The Apollo gave good entertainment, people budgeted for a twice weekly visit, it was comfortable, warm, you saw a good show with other people, and it helped them to survive until times were better. The Apollo was known in Westgate Road [where most film renting companies had their offices] **as the 'Apollo Goldmine' – it just clicked. I had a wonderful staff, and you can't run a theatre or cinema without a good staff. The greatest business we did was with Top Hat. Approximately 30,000 people paid for admission during the week …**

The auditorium of the original Apollo, 1933.

Morrison Fraser started children's matinées each Saturday at the Apollo and was known as 'Uncle Teddy' – up to 1,000 children would pack the cinema every week to see cartoons, Shirley Temple, Laurel and Hardy and to sing the Apollo songs.

Bill Whitehead, assistant manager 1935-41, remembers the showing in August 1938 of 'the latest screen novelty, Audioscopiks'. These were short films in 3-D and two-colour Technicolor. The audience was supplied with cardboard eye-masks with apertures covered in red and green/blue gelatine. One of the films had a mouse on the end of a stick being thrust into the audience, resulting in screams of horror.

When Black's Regal opened, the Apollo 'had a lady who used to go up to Black's to get the first tickets every Monday afternoon. She brought the ticket stubs back and we subtracted the [current] numbers from the [previous week's] numbers and found out how much the Regal had taken with their show that week. But I suppose Black's would have somebody who came down to the Apollo to get the first two tickets each week. We could have just rung each other up'.

In the late thirties there were over 30 staff –

Black's Regal, Shields Road, on its opening day, 3 September 1934.

five projectionists, six usherettes, four page boys, five cleaners, three cashiers, three doormen, one car park attendant, one kiosk girl, one shopkeeper and one billiard hall attendant, plus the management.

Black's Regal was the second of three large cinemas, all of this name, which were built in north east towns by Alfred Black: the others were in Sunderland (1932) and Gateshead (1937). All were among the most interesting cinemas in the area architecturally and were beautifully finished. The three Regals were never known simply as that; to the patrons of each, the name was 'Black's Regal'.

On a prominent site at the top of Shields Road, the building's frontage was finished in white stone facing with a square tower which when illuminated at night could be seen from the other side of the city. 'Lavish foyers, panelled in walnut, and metal furnishings finished in copper are provided for both stalls and circle.' The design of these foyers resembled nothing so much as a transatlantic liner of the period. Set into the terrazzo floor of the main foyer were 'elephant's footprints' in black which led from the entrance towards the paybox and the auditorium. This was Alfred Black's idea, intended as a directional guide to patrons. Within the firm laying the terrazzo, there was some confusion over how many toes an elephant had. The Regal was opened by the Lord Mayor on Monday, 3 September 1934.

After the opening of Black's Regal in Gateshead in 1937, the two cinemas normally showed films concurrently. They appeared at the Byker Regal, a second-run cinema, at the end of the three-week bar imposed by the city centre cinemas.

The Regal auditorium, 1934.

R.W. Spurs

John D. Sharp

The stage shows were never a really prominent feature and the artists rarely first-rate, although the young Bob and Alf Pearson appeared there in January 1935 and again in June 1936. J. Arnold Eagle's orchestra from Sunderland returned occasionally, but he was usually billed as an organist. The menu of the late thirties seems to have had the desired results, as the stalls were reseated in 1938, increasing capacity there to 1,247 and total capacity to 1,838.

Between the wars, the suburb of Fenham was developing rapidly. Plans for the Regal on Two Ball Lonnen, included two boxes at the rear of the stalls, but no staff or patrons can remember these, so perhaps they were not built. There was a stage and orchestra pit. The Regal was described in *Ideal Kinema and Studio* (9 November 1933) as '... an attractive hall ... The exterior is built of smooth-faced brick in keeping with the general character of the estate in which it stands...'

The Regal was opened by the Lord Mayor on 8 November 1933; the film at the opening performance was *If I had a Million* (Gary Cooper), provided by the Paramount Film Service: proceeds went to local charities. The normal run of the cinema began on the following day with *42nd Street* (Warner Baxter). The owning company was Suburban Cinemas (Newcastle) Ltd., one of Stanley Rogers' companies; the manager was James Siddons, a former Percy Park rugby

player, who stayed at the Regal until it closed. Performances were twice nightly, becoming continuous from 1935, with a Thursday programme change. Stage facilities were occasionally used for the productions of the Fenham Amateur Operatic and Dramatic Society.

The Royalty was Gosforth's second cinema, built by a company controlled by E.J. Hinge, S. Bamford and Norman Chapman. It opened on 17 October 1934 with *On the Air* (Roy Fox and his Band): proceeds went to charity. The nor-

The Regal, Fenham, August 1935.

M. Aynsley & Sons Ltd.

mal programme began on the following day with *Wonder Bar* (Al Jolson), which had been shown at the Paramount in the previous month. In 1937 the Royalty employed 27 staff: one manager, three operators (projectionists), four daymen, three cashiers, two cleaners, 12 usherettes (formerly 'girl attendants'), two page boys (one of whom was relief operator), one chocolate boy and a relief manager. The usherettes and page boys were part-time. The weekly wage bill for these 27 people was £36!

'Newcastle's new corner of entertainment' comprised the Lyric Cinema in Stephenson Road, Heaton,

Newcastle Chronicle & Journal Ltd.

Opening week at the Royalty, October 1934.

and the nearby Corner House Hotel, which opened two days later. The cinema owners were James MacHarg of Tyne Picture Houses and John Thompson. The cinema was designed by the architects of the St Gabriels Estate to harmonise with the residential character of the neighbourhood. Special attention was paid to the café which, '… in close proximity to Jesmond Dene and Armstrong Park, will, it is hoped, form a pleasureable resting and meeting place not

only for patrons of the cinema, but for members of the public generally.'

In the auditorium the predominating colour of the ceiling and walls was pink. 'Perhaps the most remarkable feature is the dado surrounding the walls of the stalls. This is about 12 feet high, and consists of a series of black and silver bands, giving a realistic effect of relief, as if the walls were completely cushioned all round … The front of the circle is picked out in pink, gold bronze and bright vermilion and the walls are enlivened by perpendicular and horizontal lines in brilliant reds and browns'. The exterior neon display was said to be the largest in the area.

The Lyric opened on 6 January 1936 with *The Little Colonel* (Shirley Temple). As might be expected with a new cinema, the first few months brought a wealth of good things: films with Ginger Rogers, Katharine Hepburn, Richard Tauber, Greta Garbo followed in quick succession to 'Heaton's Super Cinema'. But before long there was an increasing number of undistinguished double-bills and split weeks. Programming improved again when MacHarg gained sole control. *British Movietone News* was shared with the Apollo, the cans being carried between the two cinemas by a page-boy on his bicycle.

The Rialto, in Armstrong Road, Benwell, was built by the Hinge circuit and was very similar in design to the same company's Ritz at Forest Hall which had opened in 1936. 'The main elevation is modern in design, the principal features in a facade of brickwork and coloured cement being the lofty tower and the handsome metal canopies. Access is obtained via a vestibule, in which is accommodated the paybox, to the stalls foyer; 46ft. by 18ft., and lofty in proportion, this con-

Above the Lyric, February 1936. Below, the auditorium, 1936.

tributes a great deal to the favourable impression which is conveyed to the incoming patron.'

The Rialto was opened by the Lord Mayor on 10 May 1937; the first film was *Dimples* (Shirley Temple), followed in the second half of the week by *Swing Time* (Fred Astaire). The Rialto, 'Where everyone goes' had high-quality programming in its early years, but declined once the novelty had worn off.

The Embassy, on Thorntree Drive, Denton, like the earlier Plaza, Fenham and the Lyric, Heaton, was built as an integral part of a new housing estate by the developers. The *Sunday Sun* noted:

The Rialto foyer, 1937.

This is not the mere opening of an addition to the City's numerous places of entertainment. There is behind it romance, and innovation in a broader sense. Innovation, because here we have what is believed to be the first case in the area of two men who have devoted practically the whole of their partnership life to developing a given housing estate – the Thorntree Estate at Denton Bank – rounding off the job by themselves building and running its picture theatre. Romance, because Messrs. J. W. Longstaff and J. Bain are working lads, joiners to trade, who pooled their resources and comradeship in their own business venture.

At the time the Embassy was opened, the firm had sold 600 houses on the estate and were engaged on a second estate at Chapel House Farm.

There will be seating for 936 people in roomy, luxuriously-upholstered tip-up seats, a proscenium arch which will be a masterpiece in lighting with a choice of three beautiful general colour-effects, an ample free car park, a projector for plain and coloured films which is the latest type, and a scheme of decoration which is quite novel.

The latter is futuristic – but please do not get the idea that you will be confronted with daubs of red, yellow and blue in juxtaposition, representing goodness knows what.

The Embassy was opened by the Lord Mayor, Alderman John Grantham, on 6 September 1937. Advertising as 'Newcastle's Premier Suburban Cinema' with 'Trolleybus to door', the Embassy in fact programmed for a captive audience. 'A' features reached it six months after their city centre showing. A May 1939 advertisement read: 'Comfort, Courtesy, Cleanliness, plus a good show': not much confidence in the product being shown here!

The Rex, in Ferguson's Lane, Benwell Village, was built by the small local circuit owned by H.T. Smelt and opened on 8 December 1937. The facade was in sand-faced brick of two contrasting colours. An ornamental canopy with neon tubing projected eight feet over the pavement. The entrance hall and foyer walls were finished in figured walnut panelling. Additional details of the internal colour schemes were given in the local press: 'You pass through a softly-lit foyer panelled in walnut with black horizontal bands and strips of vermilion. The frieze and ceilings are in shell pink with tapering shadowgraphy. The walls [of the auditorium] are in shades of green and cream and the splay ceilings of light orange have a design in gold, cream and vermilion. Gold and orange grills appear at intervals …'

The Rex had the usual café and free car park; an integral

The Embassy, 1937.

confectionery shop was described as a 'novel feature'. As with the Rialto, programming was initially good but steadily declined.

The Gloria, in St Anthony's Road, Walker, was built for Albert Buglass, who had taken over the ailing Bensham Picture House in Gateshead in 1923 and made it a success. The name was chosen at a family meeting and was a deliberate attempt to avoid the more common cinema names. It was opened to take advantage of the large new housing estates in the area. The Gloria opened on 11 April 1938.

The entrance doors, flanked by black and gold pillars, gave onto a foyer panelled in oak with lime green stippled walls above. The floor was finished in cream and buff terrazzo. The unusual design of the auditorium was dictated by acoustical requirements. The side walls were splayed and the ceiling sloped towards the screen. It was claimed that this gave such a near-perfect result that sound-absorbent materials were only required at the rear of the hall. Above the dado the walls were decorated in a stippled hard plaster finished in autumn tints, with the fibrous relief picked out in gold, silver and turquoise. 'The ceiling is lit by a two-way trough throwing light on a plaster cove, while the large central feature, designed by the architect, consists of fibrous plaster coves which take reflected light from long metal reflectors housing strip lamps.'

The circle foyer was approached from a double curved staircase and had settees in alcoves. 'Already many comments have been made on the advantage of entering the circle from the top back instead of entrances half way up which result in the screen view being interrupted every few minutes by passing patrons'. Outside the building great trouble was taken to achieve a clean outline which could be effectively set off by tubular lighting. The stepped roof outline gave a 'waterfall' effect when the blue neons were lit at night.

Across the city, the area around the small Scotswood cinema in Bridge Crescent was quite heavily populated and the cinema was sufficiently successful for the owner to decide to rebuild. In May 1938 architect Robert Burke drew up plans for a much larger building occupying the whole of the site. The new cinema was on the stadium plan, with 112 front stalls, 220 rear stalls and 204 in a circle which was separated from the stalls by a barrier. The new cinema, the Regent, was licensed from 29 December 1938.

Above, the Gloria's neon display. Below, the auditorium, both 1938.

The decade had opened with the building of the Paramount: it closed with the city's second largest cinema, the Essoldo on Westgate Road. Built by Sol Sheckman on the site of the old Westgate Police Station, it was the fourth cinema on the street, with the Stoll, Pavilion and the Westgate its neighbours and rivals.

Essoldo Theatre (Newcastle) Ltd. was formed in January 1936, capitalised at £10,000; after the cinema had been announced, the chosen site remained vacant:

Week after week passed, and still construction was held up by lack of steel and materials and it was not until February [1938] that building operations were started, and the gigantic steel framework of the new cinema began to take shape. Since that day, many setbacks have been encountered and overcome, and twice the date of opening has had to be put back.

Rumour, less charitably, assigned the delays to Sheckman's problems in raising finance: a cinema of this size was certainly outside his experience.

[The Essoldo is] **both striking and original. Sandstone bricks and brilliant white facings give a startling effect, with the name Essoldo picked out in specially cast bright blue letters, built into the tower, on the front and at the side entrances. The unusually designed neon on the front of the building is arranged in a style never before seen in the provinces, and the amount of tubing used is the greatest in the North.**

The Essoldo, November 1938.
Inset, Sol Sheckman, c.1929.

Christopher Clavering

The Essoldo's auditorium, proscenium and Lafleur organ. 1938.

'Most important for comfort are the seating arrangements … It is expected that the Essoldo will hold 2,700 patrons in all'. This figure is pure hype, chosen presumably because it was greater than the Paramount's capacity; the cinema was licensed for 2,099. The cinema had the first all-metal screen in the North. The cinema organ was by Lafleur. The full-sized stage was fully equipped for large shows.

The first manager of the Essoldo was Hugh Le Mounier who came to the cinema from a two-year stint as manager of the Palace Theatre, Haymarket, for E.J. Hinge. He was an Australian who before the First World War had been the 'greatest strong-man act in the Southern Hemisphere.' Essoldo staff (wrongly) believed that he was the all-in wrestler 'The Blue Mask' as he was always absent on Saturday nights.

The Essoldo was officially opened on 29 August 1938 by the Lord Mayor who outlined his view of the attraction of the cinema: 'To me its great value lies in the fact that it enables our womenfolk, without having to pay undue attention to their toilet[te] and with very little expenditure of money, to live in a world of fine dresses and luxurious motor-cars and for two short hours be away in the fairylands of romance.' The women present 'laughed and applauded.'

The opening film was *The Hurricane* (Dorothy Lamour) which was also showing at the Paramount in that week. In fact the Essoldo had the same main feature as the Paramount for 15 weeks of 1939. Otherwise the programmes were rarely first-rate, with second-rank Hollywood stars topping the bill. In July 1939 Le Mounier admitted in the Essoldo's programme booklet that '… you may find names that are unfamiliar but please remember that it is the picture which is

FOR YOUR INFORMATION

Essoldo

WESTGATE ROAD, NEWCASTLE-ON-TYNE
Telephone 23232
Essoldo Theatre (Newcastle) Ltd.

Managing Director—SOL SHECKMAN.
Resident Manager—HUGH LE MOUNIER

1 p.m.	CONTINUOUS	11 p.m.

PRICES (including tax)—

| ROYAL CIRCLE 2/- | GRAND CIRCLE 1/6 | CIRCLE 1/- |
| ROYAL STALLS 1/6 | GRAND STALLS 1/- | STALLS 6d. |

Reduced Prices until 4 p.m.—
Except Saturdays and Holidays.

| ROYAL CIRCLE 1/6 | GRAND CIRCLE 1/- | CIRCLE 9d. |
| ROYAL STALLS 1/- | GRAND STALLS 9d. | STALLS 6d. |

MUSICAL INTERLUDE on the Organ
By RONALD WHITE.

CIRCLE LOUNGE CAFE
Tea and Coffee served in the Theatre

Telephone Call-box. Luxury Lounges. Free Cloaks and every attention for your Comfort and Enjoyment.

Ample Car Park arrangements in and around the vicinity of the Theatre. Thornton Street, Peel Lane, Temple Street and Sunderland Street—after 5-0 p.m.—Lights required.

Part of the Essoldo programme for June 1939.

important, not the stars.' Few thirties cinemagoers would have believed this.

The stage facilities were rarely used before the war. Gipsy Petulengro appeared in December 1938, there was a Czechoslovakian revue *Ma Vlast* in March 1939 and Younkmans and his Gipsy Czardas Band (Thrilling!, Barbaric!, Exotic!) in April. There were, as in most large cinemas, Sunday band concerts. The regular organist was Ronald White.

Newcastle had acquired 12 new cinemas in eight years, most of them built and decorated in the latest art deco style to complement the Hollywood product of the period. At a time when most homes in the city were uncarpeted and unheated, the new cinemas were warm and comfortable. Hugh Le Mounier of the Essoldo wrote in the cinema's magazine in June 1939 that: 'In winter few homes can offer so comfortable a warmth, free from draughts and with an atmosphere that is hygienically treated. In the Summer the superiority of the Essoldo even over your own home is no less marked.' These cinemas brought a new standard of luxury to suburban cinema-going. Superior types of seating, often using the newly invented 'Dunlopillo', were matched by higher standards of projection. Waiting rooms replaced queuing in the rain and snow. Front-of-house staff, including, in some cinemas, page boys employed solely to open doors for patrons, gave a new sense of style and occasion. Naturally, higher prices were asked. The most expensive cinema was the Paramount, with prices ranging from 1s to 2s 4d in the afternoon, 1s 3d to 3s 6d in the evening. Other city centre cinemas were in the range 6d to 1s 6d.

The building of all these new cinemas naturally had

Above, Poor Children's Treat at the Grey Street, Christmas 1929. Below, a page-boy at Black's Regal, Byker, c.1935.

effects on the existing picture halls, especially those in the city centre, where there were some casualties. The first of these was the Newcastle Picture House. It had been renamed the Grey Street Picture House on 5 June 1922, after a brief period as 'Picture House, Grey Street'. It was a first-run cinema throughout the twenties, sharing prime billing in newspaper advertisements with the Queen's Hall, the Pavilion and the Stoll. It was owned in 1927 by George Black and went with him to General Theatres Corporation (later part of Gaumont-British), which seems to have made little effort to support it, concentrating instead on the Queen's. The Grey Street had initially resisted talkies, its press advertising in late 1929 emphasising 'peace, tranquillity and entertainment'. It was the last major city centre cinema to convert to sound, on 28 July 1930, but by that time sound was not enough to save it. It closed on 14 May 1932 after a short life of almost exactly 18 years. The last film was *Dance Team* (Sally Eilers) and the audience filed out to 'Auld Lang Syne'. Most of the staff went to other cinemas in the Gaumont circuit. The reasons for closure were given as the 'depression, increased entertainment tax and competition'. The last is likely to be the true reason: there was no way a rather old-fashioned cinema could survive against the opening of the massive new Paramount a hundred yards away.

In 1927 the Empire in Grainger Street had been taken over by Favourite Cinemas Ltd. (later part of Associated British) and one of the cafés became a 'dance room' for a short period. Films were shown concurrently with the Grainger up the street. In October 1931 the cinema was reseated, recarpeted and redecorated but at the beginning of November 1933 its closure was announced. The lease on the building was due to expire and ABC was not interested in renewing it. The last show was on Armistice Night, 11 November 1933; the last film – shared, of course, with the Grainger – was *The Keyhole* (Kay Francis, George Brent). As the crowded cinema emptied, 'Swanee River' was played on the gramophone (the orchestra had long gone) and patrons said farewell to Bobby Cook, the commissionaire. Twelve staff were thrown out of work (though Bobby Cook went to the new Apollo).

Other older city centre cinemas remained leading venues throughout the twenties and thirties, particularly the two converted theatres on Westgate Road. In 1924 the New Pavilion was taken over by the Thompson and Collins circuit and reverted to its original name of Pavilion. Double feature first-run programmes continued throughout the twenties. A further change of ownership, to Denman Picture Houses (later swallowed by Gaumont-British) came in 1928. In November 1929 a projection box was created from the former circle bar; as this was accessed through the ladies' lounge the potential for embarrassment was high. The Pavilion was the last major city centre cinema to be converted for talkies: to complement the sound films, stage shows and cabaret, accompanied by Max Swart and his Band, were retained until January 1931; this was unusual.

After talkies, the next innovation at the Stoll was hardly as epoch-making: this was the introduction of the so-called 'Wonder Screen'. Invented by M.J. Coverdale and patented in 1930, this was a device using pulleys and shutters by which the size of the screen could be varied to suit the action. At the Stoll from 31 March, the inventor claimed that the problems of synchronising screen size and projector had been overcome. It was presumably used in conjunction with a Magnascope-type lens on the projector. Although still being advertised a year later the system was not a great success as the magnified film appeared very grainy. However, it continued to be used for newsreels only until the Second World War.

Despite the constant efforts of local management and staff to publicise programmes at the Stoll with vast posters and travelling displays, as the thirties progressed it gradually

The Stoll advertises its 'wonder screen' in 1931.

declined as a first-run cinema. Lacking the booking power of the large national circuits, which now owned the neighbouring New Westgate and Pavilion, the Stoll was reduced by the end of the decade to uninspired double-bills and reissues. The opening of the nearby Essoldo made matters worse: the Stoll had shown the very successful *Victoria the Great* in February 1938, but its successor, the Technicolor *Sixty Glorious Years*, went to the Paramount and the Essoldo in January 1939. The only, though worthy, successes at the cinema were the series of Gracie Fields pictures, although the longest run (four weeks) was of *Little Lord Fauntleroy* (Freddie Bartholomew) over Christmas 1936.

In 1928 George Black sold the Queen's Hall to General Theatres Corporation and in May the trade journal *Cinema* reported that it was to be closed for redecoration with its capacity increased from 1,400 to over 2,000 by the addition of a balcony over the existing circle. There were to be vaudeville stars as well as films. The cinema did indeed close from 23 July to 20 August 1928 and was refurbished with new seats and carpeting, but neither the balcony nor the vaudeville stars appeared (though there were some stage acts in 1928) and seating capacity in 1930 was almost unchanged at 1047 stalls, 366 circle with 170 standing.

The Queen's took all the early talkie hits. Although the cinema must have been adversely affected by the opening of the Paramount 50 yards away it remained a first-run cinema, showing the best that Gaumont-British could provide. From 1933 it was programmed in concurrency with the Pavilion, an arrangement which was maintained, with few exceptions, until 1941, when it was twinned with the Westgate.

With the Queen's Hall as the premier Gaumont house in the city, in the early thirties the Pavilion's programmes began to decline in quality, although from early 1933 it was occasionally used as an 'overflow' for the Queen's when a particularly good programme had been secured. From September in the same year the Queen's and Pavilion were run concurrently, the Pavilion taking the audience for the west end of the city.

From the early thirties the New Westgate was subordinated to the Queen's Hall (also a Gaumont theatre) in terms of programming, with many weeks of double features. On 8 February 1937 'New' was dropped from the cinema's name. From 1938, the Westgate was occasionally programmed concurrently with the Queen's, at other times showing popular films

The Pavilion auditorium, December 1960.

the week after they had played there. The Westgate continued to provide tea to patrons of matinées well into the forties; this tradition had died out elsewhere. The cynical view is that had audiences been larger, the custom would have died out even sooner.

In Byker, the Grand Theatre struggled to please everyone, still undecided on whether to be a cinema or a theatre. On 14 April 1930 the Grand showed its first talkie, *Honky Tonk* (Sophie Tucker): this spelled the end of variety with the Grand operating as a true cinema for a few years. Presumably unable to compete with both the Apollo and Black's Regal,

Gaumont-British disposed of the Grand to E.J. Hinge in 1935. Hinge continued films for a few months, closing the Grand as a cinema in March 1936 with *Boys will be Boys* (Will Hay). On 9 March it became a theatre again, with variety, plays with such local luminaries as Sal Sturgeon and in 1936, a 16-week season by the Charles Denville Famous Players – it is of this season that Kenneth More writes so hilariously in his autobiography, his main recollection being of an encounter with an incontinent camel.

Older suburban cinemas defied the challenge provided by the super-cinemas and managed to keep their audiences by reducing seat prices, installing sound and replacing wooden forms with tip-up seats. Adult prices in the smaller, older suburban cinemas were in the range 4d to 9d. The latter price would possibly buy an upholstered seat in the balcony. Although some cinemas increased seat prices to finance sound, these usually fell back to earlier levels after a few years. Lowest adult prices in 1930 were 2d at the King's, Vaudeville and the Sun. By the end of the decade of depression, these prices had increased to an average of 5d to 9½d. The cheapest cinema was now the Picturedrome, Gibson Street, at 3d. The new suburban cinemas of the thirties had prices in the range 6d to 1s.

In the early thirties demand for films was growing to such an extent that the earliest days of the picture halls were recalled by the conversion of two west end churches to cinema use. The first of these was Beech Grove Congregational Church, built in 1896 at the junction of Westmorland Road and Beech Grove, which became the Savoy. It was reconstructed for H.T. Smelt who already owned the Plaza on Westgate Road. The building was made to look less like a church by shortening two spires and masking the frontage behind cement render and stucco. But although the result resembled a cinema from the front, the building's ecclesiastical origins were starkly revealed at the sides and rear.

Originally planned to have 888 seats, the Savoy had 791 on opening. The reduction was probably due to the realisation that some sightlines from the side galleries would be dreadful (the Savoy may be the only cinema with part of its seating area

described in the plans as 'transept'). The 'modernistic' decorative scheme by Fred A. Foster of Nottingham was in the Spanish hacienda style. It is reported that the trailing vines and bunches of grapes did not survive long. The Savoy was opened on 12 December 1932 by the Lord Mayor who praised the directors' response to 'a persistent demand in the district.' The opening film was *Sunny Side Up* (Janet Gaynor), already three years old: a more recent film might have been expected at the opening of a new cinema.

St Paul's Church of England, Tindal Street, was built in 1841, became a Congregational church and was later a recre-

The Savoy, January 1968.

ation centre for the unemployed. Plans for its conversion to a cinema were drawn up in December 1932, shortly after the opening of the Savoy and possibly inspired by it. Also, the nearby Stanhope Grand had recently closed. Conversion was largely a matter of adding a brick and concrete annexe to the west end of the church, to contain a foyer with projection suite above. The original windows were bricked up but the bell-tower remained. The new cinema, called the Gem, continued to look very much like a church, particularly as it was surrounded by a graveyard complete with tombstones.

There was an unexplained delay of almost a year before the plans were announced in the press (21 October 1933); the Gem finally opened on 8 January 1934. The licensee was Sydney Millar of the Picturedrome, Gibson Street, although there is an opinion that the actual owner was a solicitor, J. Hamilton Grant. Mr McMahon remembered: 'My father J.C. McMahon retired from the army after 21 years' service in October 1933. When the Gem opened we – my father, mother, sister and I – all moved into a cottage in the grounds [the former vicarage]… From that day we all became employees of the Gem with a joint wage at the beginning of £4 10s. Later it was increased …'

The staff was: manager, commissionaire/caretaker, cleaner, four usherettes, one usher, one cashier and one projectionist with an assistant. Mr McMahon continued: 'As to myself, at 14 years of age to start with, I was chocolate and ice cream sales person, but my other chores were: taking the night's takings to the bank the following morning, collecting

The Gem, 1963.

the items sold in the kiosk from a shop opposite the Gem in Tindal Street and also selling the same items, also taking them around the cinema on a lighted tray during the performances, helping with opening and closing the cinema, drawing the stage curtains and stoking the coke boilers, and in general assisting in doing all the odd jobs as it was a family effort'.

The old church tower had horizontal blue neons at top and bottom with GEM in red neon between. Programme leaflets were hand-delivered each week to shops in the area, along with two complimentary tickets. Usherettes had to provide their own uniforms – black dress with white collar, black shoes and stockings, but the management supplied black berets with G.E.M. sewn in silver thread.

Programmes were initially twice nightly but changed to continuous from 6 pm. There were two children's matinées on Saturday, admission 2d. There were three programme changes each week. In 1934-5, in addition to films, Tuesday night was Variety Night. Later this was divided: Tuesday night became Adult Variety Night, Wednesday Juvenile Variety Night. Joe Ging remembered visits to the Gem just before the war:

A lot of snobbery went on and many locals 'wouldn't be seen dead in that dump'. An average bill would be a big picture and possibly one other, even worse than the big one, or several shorts … There were dreadful rudimentary commercials. A chorus of disapproval if – or rather when- the film snapped. By the time these films got to the Gem they were stretched to breaking point so, to a chorus of 'Missy oot!, Missy oot!', the projectionist would get on with his repair job.

There was always a talent contest – they were always precocious children who got up. If their talent had matched their cheek it wouldn't have been so painful. A typical entrant [was] the local Shirley Temple, finger curls, bow in the hair, tap shoes – the lot! Their mothers kept them in a shoe box between contests – they were never seen on the streets.

The cinemas which had been recently built adjusted fairly easily to all the newcomers. The Welbeck had to install a sound system a little over a year after it opened; the first film was *The Singing Fool* (Al Jolson) from 30 January 1930; there were two matinée performances of this and some other early talkies. 'Playhouse' was dropped from the name in January 1933, although a theatre licence was retained until 1939.

The Welbeck was several cuts above the other Walker cinemas in terms of style and comfort in the thirties: it is remembered as 'first class' and a 'beautiful cinema, it was one of the few small cinemas which had a lot of money spent on it'. The decorating was always done by professionals, not the local handymen as was often the case. In the late thirties there was a staff of about 15, including three projectionists and three cashiers – the Welbeck had separate payboxes for pit, stalls and circle.

Meanwhile in the West End, the Plaza at Fenham maintained its high quality; supporting programmes were particularly good. The orchestra went in the early years of the decade and little is heard of the organ, except in 1934 when 'interludes' were advertised. In September 1934 the Plaza was used on Sundays for interdenominational services 'to attract the crowds of young people who aimlessly throng the West Road, and to whom the ordinary place of worship makes no appeal.' (Presumably attendance at the cinema prevented them from aimlessly thronging on weeknights).

John Grantham's two cinemas on Condercum Road, Benwell had mixed fortunes. In August 1930, the Majestic Theatre went over to films and two years later the Grand temporarily abandoned films and became a theatre, opening as such on 5 September 1932 with the Denville Stock Company in *The Middle Watch*. The experiment lasted for a few weeks only and in April 1933 the Grand became a cinema again as part of the Stanley Rogers Cinemas circuit.

Under this management, the Grand continued through the thirties with long variety seasons each year, the rest of the time showing films. Douglas Gibson went to work at the Grand in 1937:

During the theatre period the screen and sound speakers were moved to the rear of the stage. I ceased to be a rewind lad but then became a general dogsbody for everyone who chose to boss me about. During the evening performances I used to work one of the lime-lights on the O.P. side. I never used to like this as it was really warm work … and if I made a slight mistake I had to go to the [artist's] room and they would give me a right dressing down.

The Majestic's auditorium, c.1937.

Actress Beryl Reid also remembers the Grand in 1937. In her autobiography she states that '…the orchestra pit was wired in – I mean, there was wire over the top of the orchestra because of all the things that the audience threw at the artists. Whenever a comic came on, there was a lady who walked about in the gallery saying, "Razor blades, buy me razor blades – she does nowt but talk." Quite a baptism!'

The Majestic Theatre opened as a cinema on 4 August 1930 with the talkie *Men without Women*. Performances were initially continuous Monday to Friday with two distinct houses on Saturday. It has been suggested that by this date John Grantham had over-extended himself financially in building the Majestic, trying to support the local dramatic society and the Denville Players and in February 1931 the Majestic was sold to the national circuit Union Cinemas. Under Union, the Majestic became Benwell's premier cinema, supplanting the Grand. Prices were reduced, while the films were good with the backing of a large circuit. The Majestic was an Union/ABC cinema until closure, films arriving there about ten weeks after their Haymarket showing.

The Jesmond was unique in Newcastle in that it served a middle-class suburb. In 1933 the cinema, which had had continuous performances since reopening, went over to 'two distinct houses' with all seats bookable. Programmes had to reflect the taste of local patrons (as in all good suburban cinemas): it was useless to expect Jesmond audiences to respond to the low farces, crime melodramas and westerns which were the staples in other parts of the city. Up-market material, such as literary adaptations, was popular, while Jeanette MacDonald musicals went down well. For example, in 1936-37, the best weekly receipts (£260) were for *Rendezvous* (William Powell) followed by *First a Girl* (Jessie Matthews);

the worst (£97) for *Sinner Take All* (Bruce Cabot) followed by *Talk of the Devil* (Ricardo Cortez).

Similarly, the Globe in Gosforth catered to more varied tastes. In December 1928 it became part of the large national circuit General Theatres Corporation. The opening of the opulent new Royalty (with which Sidney Bamford was connected) less than a hundred yards away in 1934 hurt the Globe; it did not advertise in the press and GTC seemed unwilling to support this outpost of its empire. A year later, they were probably pleased to dispose of the Globe to E.J. Hinge, who already co-owned the Royalty. Effectively running both Gosforth cinemas, Hinge was able to offer totally contrasting programmes to suit all tastes. In a move which is now impossible to understand, he left the Royalty but retained the much smaller Globe, which by the end of the thirties was often showing a stronger programme than its grander rival.

Although the Scala in Heaton continued to provide a good product, it was gradually surrounded by the new breed of super-cinema: the Apollo (1933) Black's Regal (1934) and the Lyric (1936) were all within reasonable travelling distance for Scala patrons. GTC disposed of this now old-fashioned cinema to Sol Sheckman in April 1936 and it was added to his growing Essoldo circuit. Revivals and B-features began to figure in the Scala's programmes, continuing in this vein for 20 years.

Among the older, smaller cinemas, the King's in Marlborough Crescent closed on 15 February 1930, Jimmy Lowes probably thinking the installation of a sound system not worth while. But on 17 November 1930 the cinema was open again, no longer owned by Lowes and having one of the cheapest sound systems, Electrocord. The balconies were now unused and seating was reduced to 342. The original screen, only 14 by 11 feet, remained. On the morning of 5 September 1931 the King's was destroyed by fire, only the

Newcastle Chronicle & Journal Ltd.

The King's ablaze, September 1931.

recently constructed operating box surviving. The owner, Mr Gilmartin 'had neglected to insure the place because the formation of a company to rebuild it is in progress.'

On 19 September 1918 the tiny Minerva on Byker Bank had been offered for sale and after 'spirited bidding' was bought for £2,100. It was leased to J.H. Dawe of Heaton and renamed the Imperial: Sydney Dawe was resident manager. Dawe maintained that when he took over the hall it was 'absolutely a white elephant', since he had been in charge business had boomed and he had been able to buy the cinema outright. Programmes seem to have improved by 1936, when the Imperial began to advertise in the press. Films were of good quality, but about a year old when shown there.

Early on Friday, 27 August 1937, fire broke out backstage: 'The interior was ablaze. All the walls and balcony were scorched and the talking apparatus [ie loudspeakers], valued at about £1,000 was destroyed. The projecting apparatus and the office, however, escaped damage. Mr. S. Dawe … estimated the loss at about £4,000. He said that the building had been recently redecorated and fitted with new seating accommodation.'

The Imperial reopened, seating 381, on 28 February 1938 with *Charge of the Light Brigade* (Errol Flynn). Programmes continued to be of high quality, with bright ideas like running the Andy Hardy series in sequence on successive nights.

Although not forced into it by a fire, other cinemas were redecorated and sometimes reseated in an attempt to attract and retain patrons. The Bamboro' was redecorated in the 'atmospheric style' in 1933; unfortunately no details of this are available. The Brighton on Westgate Road was reseated and redecorated in July 1934, while in 1937 the Brinkburn off Shields Road replaced the forms in the stalls and was 'beautifully redecorated'. When the Apollo opened across Shields Road in 1933, the Brinkburn benefited from the crowds turned away when that cinema was full – both were under the same management.

Advertising in the thirties characterised the Heaton Electric (which retained its increasingly anachronistic name until 1940) as 'homely and select'. The combination of cinema, dance hall and billiard hall was effective in attracting people to the complex, especially young couples. In September 1937 the Heaton closed for a week for modernisation and redecoration, reopening with *Three Smart Girls* (Deanna Durbin).

The Vaudeville, Walker, installed a sound system in 1931, but seat prices remained unchanged until the war. There were occasional variety shows in the thirties. From 1933 continuous performances were introduced; the split week continued. The newsreel, *Universal*, was shared with the Regal (Mechanics' Institute) and was three weeks out of date. In the thirties, the Vaudeville, like the Gem, was run on a day-to-day basis by a family who lived next door, the Cowens, members of whom were manager, projectionist, usherettes and cleaners. The 'Vaudie' was a little community cinema. Special matinées were held for the unemployed on Tuesdays and Thursdays. There were special prices for pensioners and as in most local cinemas there were regulars who took the same seats week after week. Staff remember that there was never any 'trouble'. The most popular films were westerns and comedies: love stories were not acceptable.

The Mechanics' Institute hall was being run by Andrew Smith in November 1931 as the Regal, but he does not seen to have lasted long. From March 1933 the Regal was licensed to by J.L. Davenport, who installed a new sound system. The final lessee, from December 1942, was John G.L. Drummond, of the Hippodrome Theatre, Bishop Auckland.

The seamier side of cinema life was evident at the Crown on Scotswood Road and at the Gaiety in Nelson Street. To judge from a letter in the *Evening Chronicle* on 26 June 1933 the Crown was a 'rough' house:

Scotswood Road, Newcastle is noted for many things, but the latest 'thrill' lies in listening to the 'rude' remarks about the following notice in the Elswick Labour Exchange window: 'Male Attendant wanted for local cinema; must be fairly well built, and able to take care of himself. Five shifts per week, includes one day off. Hours 5.45 to 10.45 daily, with Saturday matinee. Wage offered, 7s per week'. The rumour is that the one appointed must provide his own uniform and arrange for a police 'escort' on receiving his wages'.

Later in the same year, the Crown management was fined for overcrowding gangways, so business must have been good, rough or not. According to report, through the thirties and early forties the Gaiety's main clientele was 'market traders and prostitutes'; it is said that the latter occasionally 'plied their trade in the balcony and passages.'

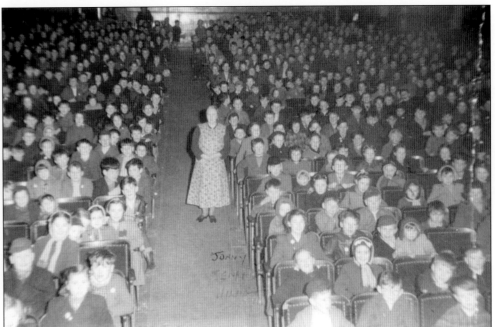

A children's matinée at the Majestic, Benwell, around 1955.

Children's matinées continued to involve the young in the cinema experience. A writer to the *Evening Chronicle* in 1970 remembered:

… queuing for the Saturday afternoon show at the Brinkburn. It was one penny to get in; when you got your ticket, you got a comic called Chips, a stick of hanky-panky, which was all colours, and a ticket with different lettering on which you had to save until you got the word 'Brinkburn'. Of course you had to swap these tickets with your friends, because the letter 'k' was always the hardest to get. I remember very well when I collected the set I had to go on the stage and I received a fountain pen.

A similar competition was run at the Raby and doubtless elsewhere.

The presents offered to children were not always of the best: at the Vaudeville in the thirties the fruit was usually bruised and the cakes were firmly believed to be misshapen rejects from a Byker bakery. Matinées at the smaller cinemas were not all sweetness and light. Les Irwin remembers the Imperial, Newburn:

… the well-off kids got into the balcony for tuppence and amused themselves by pelting orange-peel, banana skins, toffee wrappings at the less well-heeled kids in the pit. The noise of kids shouting, banging feet, fighting and creating a din was unbearable. No adults went to the matinées expecting to enjoy the film. [They] only went to chaperone small children unable to take care of themselves in the survival of the fittest conditions which existed.

The thirties saw the rise to glory of the cinema organ. Unlike those of the previous decade, these were true theatre organs with full orchestral capabilities and sound effects. The

Elton Roberts at the Paramount's WurliTzer, 1940.

city's first WurliTzer was installed in the New Westgate in 1930, imported second-hand from a cinema in the Bronx, New York. Initially used for background to advertisements and between shows, they became so popular that they were given solo spots and marquee billing. Organists at the Paramount were stars in their own right and frequently broadcast on radio.

The thirties was the great age of cinema advertising and 'stunting'. Stills boxes and newspaper publicity were considered far from adequate by the larger cinemas. Front of house displays, tie-ins with local shops, huge placards, sandwich-board men, motor cars and lorries, horses and donkeys were all pressed into service. Publicity could be taken to almost absurd lengths, as when in 1932 two 'radio masts' were erected on the roof of the New Westgate to promote an obscure film called *Are You Listening?*

The New Westgate advertises films with publicity stunts.

Above, My Old Dutch, November 1934 (photograph taken at the Oxford Galleries).

Right, Are You Listening? September 1932.

More publicity stunts: top, Call it a Day is advertised by the Queens and Pavilion, November 1937; below, Boys will be Boys at the New Westgate, December 1935; right, King Kong at the Stoll, September 1933.

8 Three news theatres: 1937

The news theatre concept, designed for shoppers and others who found themselves in the city centre with an hour or so to spare, was late in coming to Newcastle. The first news theatre in the provinces had opened in Birmingham in January 1932. The idea burst suddenly on the city, with three, the News Theatre, the Grainger and the Tatler, opening in 1937.

The News Theatre was built on the site of the Newe House in Pilgrim Street, and was opened by the Lord Mayor on 1 February 1937. Its owner was Dixon Scott (now no longer controlling the Haymarket), trading as Haridix Ltd. The opening proceeds went to the Fleming Memorial Hospital.

The programme is to last 75 minutes and will include three news reels, the latest of the cartoons, and special sport and travel films. But the great hit of the programme will be audioscopics- the new stereoscopic film entertainment in which people throw balls, push ladders and squirt soda right up to within an inch of your nose – or at any rate you think they do.

The local press also noted the provision in the operating box for the BBC's anticipated television transmissions to theatres. Programmes were continuous from 10.30 am; admission prices were 6d and 1s. Above the 402-seat auditorium

The News Theatre, Pilgrim Street, c.1938.

were coffee rooms and above them, a private cinema.

Newsreels were changed every Monday and Thursday. As the three (later five) newsreels tended to contain much of the same material, Dixon Scott junior supervised the editing of them into one sequence, choosing the best items from each; the programme was rehearsed on Sunday. After the showing, the whole thing had to be disassembled and restored to the original newsreels before they were sent on – a two-hour job for the projectionists. As the same programme was repeated up to ten times each day, the boredom threshold of staff must have been low, though there were as many as ten projectionists to mitigate this.

The News Theatre ran a competition for amateur films of the local Coronation celebrations in 1937 and a few weeks later announced the installation of a 16mm projector, inviting local amateurs to sell or hire their films for public showing. A mobile film service for factories and hospitals was also run from the cinema. Like its rival the Tatler, the News Theatre offered a venue for local film societies, normally on a Sunday; among these were The Tyneside Film Society (1949-61), the King's College Film Society (1953-54) and the Indian Association Film Society/Asian Welfare Society (1954-59). Later, societies used the private cinema upstairs.

In 1925 the Grainger cinema had been bought by Bernicia Ltd., a £1,000 company in which George Black, Sidney Bamford and James MacHarg were partners, was next leased to ABC and from 3 February 1930 showed films concurrently with the Empire down the street until the latter closed in 1933. When the enlarged and ABC-run Haymarket opened in 1936, the Grainger showed an identical programme until closure came on 31 July 1937.

NEWCASTLE'S NEWS THEATRE.
ALL PROGRAMMES ARE SUBJECT TO ALTERATION OWING TO THE VARYING LENGTHS OF THE NEWS ITEMS.
At every performance:
THE GAUMONT-BRITISH NEWS
THE BRITISH MOVIETONE NEWS
THE PATHE GAZETTE
THE PARAMOUNT NEWS

All the Week commencing December 19th.

"WILD WINGS"
An extraordinary variety of sea-birds in their mating and nesting season, on a little-known Island in Mid-Atlantic.

"NEW ZEALAND"
Beautiful scenery, including Milford Sound, and a journey across the Franz Joseph Glacier.

"WOMEN ATHLETES"
Champions of many sports.

"SPORTING DOGS"
Hunting the fox in North Carolina and shooting duck and quail: some excellent pictures of dogs retrieving game.

TWO DISNEY CARTOONS — **"MODERN INVENTIONS" "TOBY TORTOISE RETURNS"**

The News Theatre programme for December 1938.

The News Theatre foyer, 1937.

After an expenditure of about £10,000 the building reopened on 2 December 1937 as the Grainger News Theatre, part of the MacHarg circuit. The cinema, which was in very bad condition, was totally reconstructed to the designs of Marshall and Tweedy. During this rebuild, the balcony fell down, its collapse thought to have been caused by rat-runs in the timber structures. The entrance was re-faced in rough-cast pink glass with stainless steel straps. The new canopy was in coloured glass and neon; above it was a projecting sign, an inverted V in shape which was illuminated in turquoise and carried the announcement 'News Theatre'. The paybox was brought out almost to street level and the stairways altered to give easier access to the auditorium. The proscenium was brought forward to allow space for the Western Electric sound horns and ventilation system. Supporting pillars which had interfered with some sight-lines were removed and a new flat ceiling constructed. The most striking features of the re-design were 16ft. vertical lamps on each side wall and the concealed lighting effects above the proscenium.

The Grainger set out in its new incarnation to show the usual news theatre programme of cartoons, travelogues and newsreels. Programmes were continuous 12.30 until 11 pm; seat prices were identical to the News Theatre in Pilgrim Street. The whole idea was soon seen to have been a great mistake and lasted only until 26 March 1938. Perhaps it was found that 733 seats was too large for a news theatre: it cer-

The re-designed auditorium at the Grainger, 1937.

tainly could not compete on price with the newly opened Tatler, where all seats were 6d. On 28 March 1938 the Grainger reverted to a regular cinema programme and entered the most successful period of its history as a 'repertory' cinema, showing revivals and extended runs.

Last of the city's three news theatres was the Tatler at the north end of Northumberland Street, which opened on 16 December 1937. The building had originally been a café owned by Louis Bertorelli; the premises ran through the block and had an additional entrance in the Haymarket opposite the bus station. It was altered to include a 488-seat newsreel cinema with café above. By the time the Tatler opened, control had passed to E.J. Hinge.

The Tatler, Northumberland Street, 1938.

The cinema was on a single floor and was decorated by Fred A. Foster of Nottingham 'on lines of carefully restrained modernism'. On its opening day, a 'steady stream of patrons' saw a Lowell Thomas travelogue about Jamaica, a short on Salisbury Cathedral, comprehensive news coverage and one of the *Stranger than Fiction* series. Programmes were continuous from 12.30 pm until 10.30 pm. In a similar way to the News Theatre, its central location, small size and availability on Sundays made the Tatler ideal for the various film societies which began after the war.

The Tatler café c.1944 – a haven of comfort and relaxation in the war years.

9 War Years and Decline 1939-1980

On the outbreak of war on 3 September 1939 all Newcastle's 47 cinemas were closed by government order. No-one knew how long this would last and some cinemas laid off their staff. By 18 September most were open again and about to have their most profitable years, though there were three exceptions to this.

In 1927 the Royal in the Groat Market had been taken over by Stanley Rogers, redecorated and reopened as the Palladium. Through the thirties it subsisted on a meagre diet of B features. George Belshaw, who began his career as a projectionist there just before the war, remembered that most of the films were low-budget Westerns. The cinema still had gas lighting. Before each day's show, all available staff, including usherettes, had to assemble in the cellar to pull the belt of the gas engine until it chugged into life to provide power. The Palladium appears to have closed on 30 September 1939. Douglas Gibson visited it 'in the course of my duties as third [operator] at the Grand [Benwell]. It was really decrepit and used only as a storeroom and warehouse for stage scenery.' The building was used for many years as a store by provision merchants Walter Willson before being demolished in April 1963 to make way for Thomson House.

Only one cinema, the Apollo on Shields Road, was closed by enemy action. At 1 am on 6 May 1941 the cinema took a direct hit from a German bomb. Jack Ritson, chief projectionist 1933-41 recalled:

I was firewatching that night; I'd just finished the show, gone home for a snack and was back for the firewatch. There was myself, the billiard hall attendant and the father of one of the doormen. We went up onto the roof to see what was going on, of course there was a blackout, and fortunately when things got a bit heated we went downstairs into the foyer.
We hadn't sat there ten minutes before we heard one drop. We were dead lucky really. It came through the roof and hit the dress circle main girder and exploded. We were half out of the glass main doors when the canopy came down in front of us … When I got up I looked towards the cinema and flames were starting up in the stalls …

Arriving for work that morning, Bill Whitehead 'saw a crowd round the front and when I pushed through, there was no roof on the Apollo, there was a blue sky above, the radiators were hanging on the side walls with the water running out of them, a few tatters hanging where the screen had been…'

In 1931 the Adelaide in Benwell had been taken over by Union Cinemas, initially under the name of Benwell Cinemas Ltd. Union was a circuit of about 18 cinemas widely spread throughout the country, but strongest in the south and east. Advertising in the press ceased in January 1937, possibly a

sign of declining management interest. There was strong
competition from the Majestic (owned by the same company)
and the Grand; the Adelaide seems to have come a poor
third.

Despite this, some people remember that the cinema was
closed for extensive redecoration, reopened in its new glam-
orous guise, only to close permanently a few weeks later.
This oral information is in some conflict with the official
date of closure, 1 February 1943; it is unlikely that redecoration would have been undertaken during the war. The building was used as a depot by Pathé for some years, then became
a Woolworth's store.

While the fate of no other city cinema was as dramatic as
that of the Apollo, all suffered from staff shortages and lack
of maintenance. The Picturedrome in Gibson Street,
appeared in the local press only when something went wrong,
as it did in September 1942. A police inspection resulted in
S.C. Millar being fined £15 10s with costs after
Superintendent Venner 'stated that during an evening performance he failed to find a responsible person in charge.
There was no competent person in charge of the operating
box, a youth of 15 working the machines.' The cinema's
licence was withdrawn by the Watch Committee on 21
November 1942. This illustrates the difficulty of running a
small cinema in wartime when staff were not easily available.
In many cases, women were trained as projectionists to
replace the men called up to the forces.

Newcastle's cinemas emerged from the war grimy but
playing to capacity: in these years queues formed for afternoon performances. The large city centre cinemas naturally
came off best. A visit to the Paramount had always been a

*A grimy Essoldo emerges from its wartime black paint camouflage,
amidst the bunting on VE Day 1945.*

special event and now, as the Odeon, controlled since 1939 by Rank, it was undoubtedly the city's premier cinema.

During and after the war band concerts continued, to become an occasional feature later. The Odeon was the venue for lavishly produced northern and provincial premieres, when the stage facilities were used, additional lighting being borrowed from the Theatre Royal. The 'replica' Royal Film Performance of *Where no Vultures Fly* on 8 November 1951 saw a small galaxy of British and Hollywood stars – Fred MacMurray, Van Johnson, Dan Duryea, Googie Withers and Anthony Steel, on the Odeon stage.

At the rival Essoldo, programming improved greatly on the outbreak of war. The cinema's greatest triumph of this period was the first Newcastle showing of *Gone with the Wind*, which ran for four weeks from 29 July 1940. There were two showings each day at 2pm and 6pm with seat prices raised. George Belshaw remembers collecting this landmark film from the Central Station. It came with a book of instructions on how it should be shown to best advantage. Essoldo staff spent hours covering any light-reflecting surface near the screen with matt-black paint, so that nothing should detract from the film. Coffee and biscuits were served in the lounges to waiting patrons.

In the early morning of 30 April 1942 a fire was discovered in the stage area of the Haymarket: the *Evening Chronicle* reported: 'On arrival the firemen found the stage, which had a good deal of draping, ablaze and setting fire to the roof, parts of which collapsed into the pit and circle. … the fire was finally got under control after an hour as it reached the gallery end of the theatre. … The operating box and film winding rooms, with the films, were saved intact.

The walls of the building and the interior corridors were untouched.' The cinema was of course insured, but in the middle of the war there were problems in finding materials for repairs. The Haymarket was closed for over seven months, reopening on 7 December 1942 with *Mrs Miniver*. Visible fire damage after the reopening was limited to the ceiling; some seats and the plush top of the front of the circle had been patched. The lower front edge of the circle had been decorated with a band of glass 'leaves' illuminated by light bulbs; these were not replaced.

The Paramount becomes the Odeon, 1940.

Of the three Gaumont cinemas in the city, the Queen's, nearest the city centre, was favoured over the Westgate and the Pavilion. The Pavilion, which had for years been 'twinned' with the Queen's, taking the audience for the western half of the city, was supplanted by the Westgate in April 1941. The Pavilion was left to pick up whatever remained in the way of reissues and second runs and later shared bookings with the Odeon. Its gallery was closed in March 1949.

A bevy of Odeon usherettes, October 1947.

During the war the Stoll specialised in second runs of films which had initially appeared elsewhere in the city. *Gone with the Wind*, which had opened at the Essoldo in 1940, came to the Stoll with runs of seven weeks in 1942 and four weeks in 1943. For some reason, the Stoll did acquire the first run of the Gary Cooper/Ingrid Bergman *For Whom the Bell Tolls* in 1943.

The peak year for cinema attendances in Britain was 1946; from then on there was an initially slow, but accelerating decline. The halcyon days had gone forever as cinemagoers replaced obsession with discrimination. Gradually through the fifties all sorts of factors worked against the cinemas. Living conditions improved so that the local cinema was no longer warmer or more comfortable than most homes. After the war, many cinema owners did not spend money on redecorating their cinemas and they gradually became dowdy and unattractive. Even when cinemas were redecorated, as with the Odeon (former Paramount) in 1949, they were cheaply done, in keeping with those times of austerity, with little attempt to retain their thirties glamour and magic.

The major cinemas came through the years after the war largely unaffected: not so the smaller city and suburban venues. The doubling of entertainment tax during the war (introduced as a temporary wartime measure in 1916!) affected them badly. These halls, owned by families or small local circuits, fell victims to financial pressures from all directions.

In the late forties the Gaiety in Nelson Street was an 'overflow' for the other city centre cinemas. When they put the 'house full' signs up, people went to the Gaiety rather than go home without seeing a film. It was a 'little gold-mine', with queues every Saturday night. It may have been these crowds which attracted the licensing authorities to the Gaiety. A renewal of its licence was deferred pending an inspection on 18 February 1949. The poor exit facilities were noted as well as the fact that inflammable material was stored in the warehouse below. The emergency exit was agreed by an ex-member of the Gaiety (nicknamed the 'Pie and Tatie') staff to have been dreadful, consisting of a rickety cast iron staircase to the alley below. But it had been so for years, and this seems to have been a case of a new broom sweeping clean. A deputation from Stanley Rogers Cinemas to the city council proposed substantial alterations but in May it was decided that these would be uneconomic and the cinema stayed closed. The Regal, Walker, closed after a similar inspection on 26 February 1949.

For other cinemas, there was not a sudden closure by safety authorities but rather a gradual decline. Bill Rosser recalled that at the Grand, Benwell, most seats had lost their fixings to the floor. Programmes were mostly aimed at children with Roy Rogers westerns and cliff-hanger serials. At quiet moments the thumping of the engine which still provided the cinema's power could be heard. From 1953, three-month licences were applied for and the hall does not seen to have been licensed at all for most of 1954. It finally closed on 29 September 1956. Likewise the Vaudeville, Walker, which closed so abruptly on 2 August 1958 that staff were unable to retrieve personal possessions from the building, and the Regent, Scotswood, which shut 'owing to lack of business' on 6 July 1957.

Various innovations of American origin such as 3-D and Cinemascope failed to halt the decline. The gimmicks could

Queues for The Jolson Story at the Essoldo, October 1948. (The first 19 weeks of the run had been at other cinemas.)

Turners Photography, Tyne & Wear Archives

not disguise the fact that films of the fifties were generally of lower quality that those of the two previous decades. All agree, however, that the major reason for the decline of the cinemas – especially those in the suburbs – was the introduction of commercial television by Tyne-Tees in January 1959. The statistics of cinema closures in the city bear this out: 1958, two; 1959, three; 1960, seven; 1961, seven (see table). The suburban cinema audience was the first to switch allegiance to television. When a local cinema closed, its patrons did not, by and large, transfer their custom to the next nearest cinema; they gave up their regular cinema habit altogether, so the loss of audiences was cumulative. In the fifties, the TV was a major item of purchase. Those who took the plunge wanted to get value for their money in terms of hours watched.

Cinemas were suddenly vulnerable: they seemed to lose out to every new trend and fashion. Later in this period, the Betting and Gaming Act of 1960 dealt two more body blows in the form of bingo and nightclubs. Bingo, particularly, appealed to a large part of the traditional cinema audience. When the Regal, Fenham, closed on 30 April 1960, its first and last manager, James Siddons told the *Evening Chronicle*: 'The reason for the dwindling audiences is television and in particular commercial television. Attendances dropped as soon as Tyne-Tees Television began transmitting in January last year. Another reason is housey-housey, which has been started in many of the surrounding church halls. This has taken away most of our female audience.'

Some cinemas, like the Crown on Scotswood Road, tried to combine films with bingo; it was usually bingo which survived, except at the Apollo and the Jesmond. The night clubs

The effects of television – post-war closures
(Tyne Tees TV opened in January 1959)

Gaiety	26 February 1949
Regal, Walker	28 February 1949
Grand Theatre	27 August 1954
Grand	29 September 1956
Regent	6 July 1957
Vaudeville	2 August 1958
Gaumont (Westgate)	29 November 1958
Raby	7 March 1959
Bamboro'	11 April 1959
Lyric, Heaton	20 June 1959
Grainger	26 March 1960
Regal, Fenham	30 April 1960
Embassy	25 June 1960
Brinkburn	2 July 1960
Picturedrome	20 August 1960
Gem	29 October 1960
Plaza	31 December 1960
Prince of Wales	?1960
Olympia	8 April 1961
Imperial, Newburn	13 May 1961
Majestic	20 May 1961
Heaton	17 June 1961
Rialto	25 June 1961
Scala	1 July 1961
Globe	25 November 1961
Gloria	4 March 1962
Crown	24 November 1962
Brighton	20 April 1963
Imperial, Byker	24 August 1963

The Queen's Cinema in 1958. While suburban cinemas closed across the city the Queen's series of blockbusters kept the crowds happy (Con Docherty, manager, at left).

which opened in Newcastle in the sixties merely took away another part of the audience. For the surviving small cinemas, the youth culture explosion of the same decade often meant vandalism. Cars, foreign holidays and DIY in new homes mopped up surplus cash.

By the end of 1963, only a handful of suburban cinemas had survived the carnage. The unlikeliest such was the Savoy, Westmorland Road, which had become part of the Essoldo circuit in 1948 and was allowed to decline. A visitor in 1965 noted that the auditorium was painted in orange and blue, probably years before. Silver stars stencilled on the blue could just be made out. After a freak storm damaged the roof in December 1965, it was in such a poor state of repair that its licence was temporarily revoked. Now recognised as the worst Essoldo cinema, the Savoy was open again when, on 29 May 1966, a fire broke out in an adjoining store room. The Savoy closed and was vandalised. After much expense, Essoldo reopened it as a bingo club in October 1969. It was finally burnt down on the night of 26-27 May 1997.

In 1954 the Rex, Benwell Village, like the Plaza, was sold to W.J. Clavering. With the Rialto closed from 1961, the Rex lasted much longer than most suburban cinemas, although programmes in the late fifties and early sixties were almost vintage. Owned by Consett Cinemas Ltd. from November 1963, the Rex was showing childrens' matinées as late as 1965. There was constant trouble with what were then known as 'unruly teenagers'. The cinema closed on 10 August 1968 and is now a social club.

In January 1954, when Cinemascope was introduced at the Odeon with a 5-week run of *The Robe*, the Welbeck advertised films on a 'panoramic wide screen.' This was presumably achieved by fitting a larger screen, with masking top and bottom, and must have led to the loss

The Rialto as a bingo hall, 1963.

of some of the picture; certainly the films advertised during the few weeks of the experiment were in the conventional 4:3 ratio. Showing a mixture of Rank and ABC releases, the Welbeck outlasted most suburban cinemas. There were the usual sixties problems with vandalism, a steel bar being hurled through the screen one night in May 1964. A bingo licence was refused in May 1966 but allowed the following year and the Welbeck was last licensed as a cinema on 6 December 1968. It became a full-time bingo club run by the Noble Organisation, its attractive tiled facade masked behind blue metal cladding. It remains a bingo club, though under different ownership.

Sometimes the real estate was far more valuable than the cinema which occupied it, especially in the city centre. Due to the foresight of one of its directors, the company which owned the Grainger had purchased the cinema's street frontage in 1948. When in 1960 Dunn's the hatters bought the premises, they paid an estimated £600,000 for it. With sums of this magnitude being offered, it is small wonder that cinema owners were willing to sell up.

Only one cinema owner had sufficient confidence in the future to actually build a new cinema in the fifties. This was James MacHarg of Tyne Picture Houses, who rebuilt the Apollo on Shields Road, bombed in 1941. For years after the war the remains of the Apollo were a vast advertising hoarding. The billiard hall was not affected by the bombing and continued as such until after the war; it then became successively a soft furnishing factory and a clothing factory. In June 1947 steel was not available for the rebuilding. Further attempts were made in 1950 and 1953, the latter being stopped when the city council declared that the site was required for a new link between Shields Road and Tynemouth Road. Finally, in 1955, permission was given to rebuild the Apollo to its 1933 plan, as required by the War Damage Commission.

The new Apollo opened on 19 March 1956. Admission prices ranged from 1s 6d (front stalls) to 2s 6d (Royal circle); pensioners paid 9d. Still an independent cinema, the Apollo played films from the National (ie films Rank didn't want) and ABC releases a few weeks after the city centre. Part of the cinema was used by 'Nova Signs', one of James MacHarg's companies which made pub signs. On 17 September 1962, although the cinema was trading successfully, its owners decided that bingo would be more profitable and closed it.

The chief projectionist, Mannie Moorhouse, stayed on to

Right above, the Apollo, Shields Road, 1956.
Below, the Apollo Entertainment Centre, 1973.

Tom Oxley, courtesy of E. Moorhouse

maintain the bingo equipment and the bandits, meanwhile keeping the projectors cleaned and oiled. His foresight was rewarded when in June 1964 the Apollo was taken over by Arnold Sheckman, who reopened it as a cinema on 2 August with *The Nutty Professor* (Jerry Lewis).

The cinema was bought by the Classic Group in January 1972 and closed for tripling on 1 October. Cinema 1 opened to the general public on 30 December with *Mary, Queen of Scots* (Vanessa Redgrave). Late shows, commencing at 10.45 pm were begun. The triplets were born (as the advertising put it) on 26 December as the Apollo Entertainment Centre. Cinema 1 was the former circle; 2 and 3 were created from the stalls area. Seating capacities were 534, 180 and 169; all seating was new with greater leg-room and better sightlines. A licensed bar was added; total cost was reported as £100,000. On 5 February 1973 a fourth screen (87 seats) was added in what had been the stalls waiting area. Cinemas 2, 3, and 4 had a single projection suite.

The fourth screen did not last long. It started as a club cinema, was then opened to the general public and ended as a skateboard centre; it was empty by 1980. In 1975 a bingo licence for Cinema 1 was refused; a slow decline began. By the early eighties shows were evenings only, with the cinema closed on Tuesdays. There was one projectionist, with part-

E. Moorhouse

The Apollo auditorium. The features on the side walls are reminiscent of the original Apollo.

time help. Various ideas to save the Apollo were discussed, such as closing Cinema 1 and operating only the two minis, but head office decided on closure.

The Apollo Entertainments Centre closed on 1 October 1983; the final film in Cinema 1 was *Friday 13th Part III*. The building was offered for sale until September 1989, when it was opened by Autospray as a car maintenance centre. The foyer was attractively redesigned, but the most eye-catching feature of the building was the rear half of a red mini car protruding from the facade. The building was demolished in December 2001.

The Royalty, Gosforth, survived the television/bingo

onslaught of the fifties and sixties by showing films a few weeks after the city centre at cheaper seat prices. It also had its devoted local patrons. But by the mid-seventies, time had caught up with the Royalty. In November 1974 its owners, still the Royalty (Gosforth) Ltd., with Donald Chapman as chairman, proposed to demolish the cinema and replace it with a five-storey entertainments complex with restaurant, sports facilities, offices and a mini-cinema. This plan was rejected by the city council and in September 1975 an enquiry was held into it, along with an alternative which was to convert the ground floor into a store with a cinema retained in the circle. Both schemes were turned down by the Environment Secretary on the grounds of 'overdevelopment' of the site.

The Royalty struggled into 1977, being offered for sale for £25,000 in April. Later that year several schemes were put forward: the cinema was to become a Hindu temple, a freezer centre or a music hall with twin cinema. Finally in June 1978 the Royalty was bought by Whitley Bay Entertainments (owners of the Spanish City) who proposed the conventional solution of a bingo club. Objections came from local residents and from the owners of the Globe, which 'amply supplied the need for a bingo hall in Gosforth.' By October the owners had agreed to include a luxury cinema in the former circle. Opposition continued.

The Royalty, throughout all this debate, was still a cinema, although with decreasing success. A newspaper report in May 1980 logged audiences of 19 and 11 at showings of *Rising Damp* (Leonard Rossiter): perhaps not a fair test as this film failed everywhere. Ownership had now passed to Paul Burton who managed Dexy's Midnight Runners and

The auditorium at the Royalty, September 1959.

Turners Photography, Tyne & Wear Archives

owned a chain of hairdressing salons. Under temporary licences, the Royalty became a venue for occasional pop concerts but a full licence was refused by the magistrates on the grounds of noise. By October 1981, apart from school holidays, only the circle was in use. Despite an appeal, a licence was not granted and the cinema closed on 30 December 1981. The building was put on the market at £80,000. The interior was vandalised. The site and building were bought by developers Longbarr who demolished the Royalty in May 1984 and built flats on the site.

By the outbreak of World war II, the Jesmond was booked as part of the MacHarg circuit, along with the Apollo and the Lyric, Heaton. While other suburban cinemas fell to television around 1960, the Jesmond kept going, supported by vast numbers of students living in bedsits in the area. It was also helped by ease of its access by rail and its very reasonable prices.

In 1963 it was taken over by Arnold Sheckman and had bingo one night per week, although it continued to be patronised as a cinema. By 1974 it was owned by Sheckman's Dorlyn Entertainments, who in April proposed a change of use to 'cinema and/or bingo'. Petitions were organised in support of cinema use: '… there is great concern over the possible loss of an amenity which the residents, both in Jesmond and other parts of the city, value highly and most affectionately for its varied family entertainment.'

Although the residents won this fight, there was concern that the defeated owners would allow the building to decay and the city council agreed to allow bingo on not more than four nights a week. In fact, the new licence was not taken up and Dorlyn sold the Jesmond to the 'Perthshire based bingo specialists Top Flight Leisure in July 1975. The battle recommenced, but from 6 October films were shown on only Tuesday, Wednesday and Sunday evenings and Saturday afternoon. Dual use did not last long. In January 1977 the Jesmond was bought by Prem Khanna, who abandoned the bingo sessions.

The Jesmond continued as a full-time cinema; in 1978 the 800-seat cinema was attracting 400-500 people each night for films only two weeks after the city centre and at cheaper seat prices. Although the Jesmond defied time, by the early 1990s the opening of the Warner multiplex had affected audiences to the extent that the small staff sometimes outnumbered patrons. The cinema closed on 1 October 1993, although the building still stands.

Through the fifties Black's Regal in Byker traded successfully, with audiences coming from other parts of the town to this immaculate cinema. Seats were cheap when compared with the city centre and according to Bob Spurs, manager 1949-72:

it was just as good entertainment; sometimes better, there was the organ, the occasional stage show, the newsreel, an interest film and the big film – sometimes a double feature. You had Byker area and Wallsend – you could say they were more or less your stalls patrons. Heaton, Jesmond, they were your circle patrons. [There were] two classes of audience, but they were both marvellous, they loved their cinema.

In November 1955 the Regal was taken over by the Rank Organisation and renamed Odeon; it had been programmed by Rank for some time. In 1956 the Apollo reopened as an apparent competitor, normally taking the ABC release, but '…we never found that the Apollo was a great competitor. It never seemed to make much difference unless [it had] something really outstanding. The Odeon seemed to keep its patrons. They had their own seats and the staff knew them.'

The Byker Odeon closed on 11 November 1972; the last film was *How to Steal a Diamond* aka *The Hot Rock* (Robert Redford). An application for a bingo licence was refused in May 1975. A supermarket, the Byker Superstore, opened briefly in the gutted building. It was demolished early in 1987; a petrol filling station now occupies the site.

Cinemascope and the other special

The Jesmond, 1965.

systems introduced in an attempt to stem the decline in attendances, had more impact in the city centre cinemas. Of the three ex-Gaumont cinemas, now owned by Rank, two survived into the seventies and eighties. The third, the Westgate, renamed Gaumont on 10 July 1950, was a victim of the rationalisation which accompanied the final merger of the Odeon and Gaumont theatre groups and closed on 29 November 1958. Rank then turned the building into the Majestic Ballroom, opening on 26 February 1959, but this failed to make any headway after the rival Mayfair opened.

After the Odeon/Gaumont merger, the Pavilion occupied a position behind the Odeons at Newcastle and Byker, but instead of final closure, the Pavilion was given a new lease of life by Rank in the form of modernisation. According to the manager, reported on 3 January 1961, it was to have first runs of outstanding feature films. All the Edwardian elegance of boxes and statues of naked ladies was ripped out or masked behind acoustic tiles. It was a conversion very much of its time: an effective but soulless auditorium was created.

The cinema was now used for extended runs in a rather

pale reflection of the Queen's. The longest run at the Pavilion was *Lawrence of Arabia* in 1963 (20 weeks), which had transferred from the Queen's. It was during this run, on 2 August, that part of the ceiling fell on the audience, causing cuts, bruises and shock to 30 people. There were luckily no serious injuries. The ceiling fall was apparently caused by vibrations from work in an adjoining building; the cinema reopened in the following week.

On 4 March 1968 the Pavilion was again closed for modernisation, opening on 28 April as a 'showcase' cinema. New lighting, a new screen and new seating in tangerine were installed. But at the end of 1975 the closure of the Pavilion was announced. A spokesman for Rank explained that it had been known for some time that the future of the cinema would be suspect after the tripling of the Odeon: 'At the moment we have five screens in Newcastle, and we can't always get the right sort of films to show. We are always sorry to see a cinema go, but places are always under scrutiny if they can't pay their way. The Odeon in Newcastle is thriving. With the Queen's and Pavilion that makes three and you can't keep three large buildings of that order going.'

Closure came on 29 November 1975. The building then began to decay: a proposal in 1984 to convert it into a restaurant and night club came to nothing. The building (apart from the frontage) was demolished in 1990; flats were proposed for the site. There were further delays; finally the frontage was demolished in May/June 1992 and the block of flats built.

The Queen's in Northumberland Street was the third former Gaumont cinema in the city. The association of the Queen's with spectaculars and extended runs began late in

The Pavilion's final canopy, April 1968.

1957 with Mike Todd's *Around the World in 80 Days*. The original narrow proscenium arch was clearly inadequate for a wide-screen process, so a new flat screen was erected on a scaffolding framework in front of it. The old organ was sold for £25 and removed. *Around the World in 80 Days* ran from Boxing Day 1957 until 22 March 1958. A small orchestra of seven played each day: it had been discovered that the presence of live performers meant an abatement of entertainment tax which paid for the orchestra and gave a profit besides. After the end of this run, twinning with the Westgate recommenced (apart from a season of Cecil B. de Mille's *The Ten Commandments* from May to August 1958); a new Todd-AO installation was completed in September and the number of front stalls seats reduced.

The film which made the Queen's reputation as an extended run cinema was *South Pacific* which opened on 22 September 1958 and closed 81 weeks later on 9 April 1960. During this run it was rumoured that the cinema was to be converted into a dance hall, but it was contracted to Fox for the run and it was the Westgate which met this fate.

Long runs were interspersed with single week performances until on 15 June 1963 the Queen's closed for conversion to a Cinerama Theatre. The 50-year old cinema was gutted and internally reconstructed by main contractor Stephen Easten. The roof was removed and a new one constructed 12 feet higher to accommodate the 28 feet high screen. The old projection box was removed from behind the circle, which was totally rebuilt with its own foyer. 'Wall decoration, seating and curtains tone in with each other, and the general level of lighting ensures that no particular surface will be highlighted, thus focusing the viewer's attention on the screen without any distraction of the eye.'. The cost of the operation was reported as £175,000. Seating was reduced to 972 (613 stalls, 359 circle).

The Queen's Cinerama Theatre opened on 9 November

Above, the Queen's auditorium, November 1957.
Below, the Queen's Cinerama auditorium, November 1963.

1963 with *How the West was Won*. 'A realistic effect was introduced in the foyer, where a small 'Hill Billy' band played lively music, and about 30 members of the Newcastle Amateur Operatic Society disguised as cowboys, Red Indians, and Western characters, sold programmes.'

Three-lens Cinerama was not a great success, the opening film running until 23 May 1964 and being followed by only two others in this process, *Cinerama Holiday* and *The Wonderful World of the Brothers Grimm*. At the end of September the cinema was closed for a week for the installation of single-lens Cinerama equipment, which was first used for *It's a Mad Mad Mad Mad World*. It was found that this lens could show films shot in 70mm without distortion; thus paving the way for the Queen's longest run, *The Sound of Music*, 140 weeks from 18 April 1965.

In 1968 Rank introduced Multiple Unit Management, under which the Queen's was subsidiary to the Odeon, with interchange of staff. By 1978, with the Odeon tripled, rumours of the imminent closure of the Queen's began. Littlewoods, whose store was adjacent, planned to develop the site. In January 1979 a Rank spokesman said: 'It has been obvious for some time that a lot of money would have to be spent on the cinema to bring it up to modern standards. Although it will be a shame to lose the historic building of the Queen's, we have to face the reality that the money would probably be better spent on a completely new cinema.'

This took the form of the addition of a fourth screen to the Odeon complex. The Queen's closed on 16 February 1980 with *One Flew Over the Cuckoo's Nest*. After remaining empty for a few years, the building was demolished in February 1983 and an (ultimately unsuccessful) shopping

Newcastle Chronicle & Journal Ltd

Two concerned citizens protest at the showing of Luchino Visconti's Rocco and his Brothers at the Stoll in January 1962. The cinema commissionaire in the background was the last of his kind in the city.

arcade built on the site. This was later converted into gaming areas and cafés.

The Stoll had perhaps the most interesting fate. In the 1950s, as the only cinema in a theatre circuit, it had an increasingly idiosyncratic booking policy, taking films from small distributors who were usually ignored by the majors (often with good reason). Films were booked at head office in London and by the early fifties were usually of the X-certificate horror variety. Interspersed with these were British and French comedies. Later in the decade came the first of the 'sex' films for which the Stoll became notorious.

The Stoll caters for its particular audience in 1962.

All this is well-known: what is less well remembered is that in the years before the Tyneside Film Theatre, the Stoll introduced Newcastle audiences to the best in continental films of the time. No other cinema would touch films directed by Malle, Bergman, Resnais or Visconti. It would be naive to assume that the Stoll management's intention was to broaden the cinema education of its patrons, but that was the result.

Through the sixties and into the seventies, as the grip of censorship slackened, Stoll programmes became increasingly soft-porn. Closure of the cinema was announced on 30 January 1974. Stoll Theatres Corporation announced that attendances had fallen over the last year and the Stoll had been losing money for some time. The manager said that the cinema had been doing exceptionally well until a few years ago with its programmes of sex and horror films. He thought the flood of X and AA certificated films on to the market was the cause. People had not become less interested in these films, but 'more cinemas were jumping on the bandwagon.' In a sense, the Stoll was a victim of its own success in its particular corner of the market: more of its typical product was now on general release. The cinema was old, lacking the facilities and comfort of newer buildings like the Studios complex around the corner.

The Stoll closed on 23 March 1974 with, true to the last, two X-certificated films, *World Without Shame* and *Danish Bed and Board*. There was immediate concern that the 107 year old theatre should be preserved. After many problems had been overcome, the Stoll reopened as the New Tyne Theatre in April 1977. Reverting to its original name of Tyne Theatre in November 1986, it was later renamed the Newcastle Opera House, presenting live shows only, and is now the Journal Tyne Theatre.

One reason for the closure of the Stoll was the appearance of a rival a hundred yards away in 1973. The Leeds-based Star Group of Companies specialised in opening entertainment complexes in major cities. The Newcastle Entertainment Centre, in part of a massive 1933-built Cooperative Society block in Waterloo Street called Alfred Wilson House, comprised, in addition to a 4-screen cinema, a Hofbrauhaus ('bringing fun-loving Munich to Newcastle'!!) and a disco called Scamps. The complex opened on 13 December 1973.

Studio 1-2-3-4, March 1983.

The four auditoria were all small; although basic in design, all the equipment was brand-new. There was a single projection room with four Westar 5000s and four Westrex towers. Using electrically interlocked synchronous motors and a series of rollers, all auditoria could show the same film if necessary. Star policy was to show contrasting programmes in the cinemas, but soon most were occupied by either sex or horror films. Studio 1, the smallest auditorium, opened on 30 March 1980 as the Penthouse Cine Club, showing uncensored films. After almost ten years, the Studios closed on 26 March 1983. The whole building, including the former cinemas and the nightclub, latterly known as Rockshots, was converted to loft apartments in 2003-5.

The Tyneside Film Theatre, 1971.

W. Harle

The Tyneside Cinema in the 1990s.

When, in the late sixties, cinema newsreels were successfully challenged by television news programmes, the two remaining news theatres underwent very different fates. The News Theatre in Pilgrim Street closed, opening on 17 March 1968 as the BFI-supported Tyneside Film Theatre. The first film was the controversial Swedish sex comedy *Hugs and Kisses*. The Film Theatre closed in 1975 but reopened with new financial backing in the following year as the Tyneside Cinema. Since then, the frontage of the cinema has been remodelled several times but the auditorium is almost perfectly preserved and was listed Grade II in 2000. At the time of writing major restoration work, as well as new screens, is proposed.

Above left, the auditorium, after restoration as the Tyneside Cinema, 1989.
Left, the first floor landing.
Above the Tyneside Cinema unveils its new canopy, 2004.

By contrast, the Tatler had a long drawn out fall from grace. In July 1964 it was bought by Classic Cinemas Ltd. who fitted a new cinemascope screen, installed a Projectomatic system and redecorated the café. In 1969 the news theatre era ended in the city: the Tatler was one of only four or five left in the country. Classic announced that from 9 November the Tatler – now renamed Classic – would begin an extended run

The Tatler's last days as a cartoon cinema, 1965.

of Peter Fonda's *Easy Rider*. Newcastle citizens were not to be alarmed: 'we have had very large audiences of hippies [at the Classic, Piccadilly] and, personally, I have found them very charming people, and they have caused no trouble.'

From 20 September 1970 the Classic began a new life as a cinema club for members only, apart from a Saturday morning family show and late-night shows (which had begun in July 1969). Seating was re-spaced and reduced to 418. Again, people were reassured: 'If someone wants to see three hours of pornography they will be disappointed. All the films come well within the law.' On its first anniversary, the club claimed 6,000 members and from November 1971 there was to be a monthly striptease presentation.

Striptease was hardly new to the north-east, but the fact that it was taking place in a cinema aroused press interest. A reporter found the cinema packed for the stripper: the films

were *Double Initiation* and *The Nude and the Prude*. Perhaps in protest, the cinema heating had failed that morning. The cinema was renamed the Tatler Cinema Club in February 1972. By 1975, although club membership was said to be 10,000, interest was falling. A reporter visited a performance at which the audience for lunchtime striptease was about 50 – 'the cinema seemed empty and strangely silent.' His attempt to interview patrons ended when he was told to '**** off'.

In October 1975 and again in 1978 plans were announced to convert the cinema to shops, but it plodded on. In July 1979, after the Classic chain had been taken over by Lord Grade, there was a feeling that the club shows might cease, as had happened in Leeds, but 'We won't be playing the As and AAs at the Newcastle Tatler because too many cinemas there would get them before us. There's no money in that.'

But the change did indeed occur when on 4 November 1979 the cinema opened to the general public as the Classic. It was not saved, however, closing on 24 August 1980. Shops and a bank now occupy the site.

The Classic's Haymarket entrance, c.1970.

E. Moorhouse/ Tom Oxley

10 Way out west – the Newburn area

The picture halls and cinemas in the villages and towns on the western outskirts of Newcastle were different in size and style from those of the city. With smaller areas and population from which to draw their audiences, they were more modest, with a greater use of 'temporary' wood and corrugated iron structures (large huts, really) which could easily be taken down and reused elsewhere if the picture hall was unsuccessful.

The first picture hall in the villages to the west of Newcastle was the Picturedrome and Variety Palace, Newburn, licensed from 5 October 1910, initially for six months only. It was at the lower end of Westmacott Street at its junction with Grange Road and was a temporary building in wood and corrugated iron, 58 feet long by 48 feet wide. A wooden lean-to contained the tiny foyer with projection box above. There was one toilet, behind a curtain to the right of the screen! A surviving photograph of a large group of entertainers appearing here suggests that variety acts were more important than picture shows. The owner was Marshall J. Rutter, a Lemington housepainter. When he moved his interest to the new picture hall at Lemington in 1911, the

Picturedrome was taken over by Thomas R Fyall, but soon closed, presumably because of overwhelming competition from the newly-built Imperial along the road.

Marshall Rutter opened a hall in Tyne View, Lemington, between Sugley Street and Rokeby Street on behalf of Roy C. Dunford, a Newcastle chartered accountant. He successfully applied for a licence from 18 October 1911. 'The Sunday

A group of artistes appearing at the Picturedrome, Newburn in 1910. Some are showing a raised middle finger which presumably had a different meaning in those days!

evening entertainment' he said rather sanctimoniously 'would commence and finish with the singing of hymns.' Almost nothing is known about this picture hall, except that it was a timber framed structure covered in painted corrugated iron, a style much favoured in the western suburbs, and Dunford agreed to remove it within six months if requested to do so. According to its plan, it had no toilets!

The first owner of the Imperial Electric Theatre on Station Road, Newburn, was Towyn Thomas: the picture hall was licensed from 18 October 1911. Seating was initially 550, but the next owner, William B. Saul, who took over in August 1912, increased this in July 1913 by the addition of a 131-seat gallery and the removal of some of the 'select' tip-up seats in the stalls and their replacement with forms. This increased capacity to 720. In January 1919 Thomas Maughan, a railway locomotive driver from Blaydon, took over the hall; in that year *Northern Lights* reported that business was so good that people were being turned away and two shows nightly were found to be necessary.

Samuel R. Piper was a Cornishman who began his working life as a miner and became deputy overman at Pegswood Colliery near Morpeth. In about 1898 he went as deputy to North Walbottle Colliery, where he remained until 1912, when he left a secure job for the risks of cinema ownership. The Picture Palace was in Stamfordham Road, Westerhope, and was basic: as built it had stalls seating only, with the exception of a tiny balcony seating 16 to the right of the projection box. The cinema seated 450 and was licensed from 14 August 1912.

A private limited company called the Throckley Picture Co. was formed with £500 capital in September 1912 by

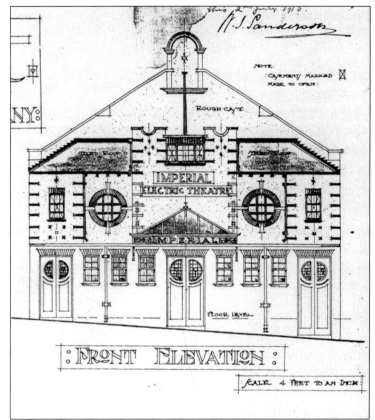

The architect's elevation of the Imperial, 1913.

Towyn Thomas and H.S. Armstrong. This company built the Picture and Variety Palace. It was a temporary corrugated iron building, 70 feet long and 45 feet wide, just off the main Newcastle to Hexham road. Most of it was, in fact, the former Picturedrome from Newburn, dismantled and transported to Throckley by Towyn Thomas in October 1912 and a further 12 feet added to its length. It was licensed from 12 November 1912. There were several licensees before 1919, including S.O. Armstrong, who owned the Britannia, High Westwood and John Cheeseman, who later managed cinemas at Chopwell and Rowlands Gill. No details of programmes are available, but singing competitions were held every Friday night, the winner receiving 2s 6d. A client of the Grange Day Centre remembers that the hall had no proper entrance: a curtain was pulled across when the show began. Pictures were shown once nightly, with three changes weekly. Seating was about 600.

In view of the flammability of nitrate film and the fact that most of the audience smoked and casually discarded their stubs, fires in cinemas were happily rare: an exception was the Picture and Variety Palace. In July 1922 the hall was taken over by an ex-officer, Charles Nicholl, who (presumably) renamed it the Imperial. Unluckily for him, early on Tuesday morning, 12 December 1922, the cinema was destroyed by fire. The Imperial was a mass of flames when the Newburn Fire Brigade arrived, but they prevented the fire spreading to the nearby Throckley Cooperative Hall and other buildings in this 'congested neighbourhood'. The cinema's dynamo and gas engine, as well as Nicholl's personal belongings, were destroyed.

Nearly two years later in August 1924, Thomas Charlton of Sugley Villas, Lemington, a builder and funeral director, submitted plans for a new cinema on the site. Designed by W.H. Burrows, this was another 'temporary' building, with side walls and roof of corrugated iron. There was a stage, two dressing rooms and a small balcony and operating room. But was this cinema ever built? The evidence suggests that it was not: there is no record of a licence being granted and it was never listed in directories. At this time, Thomas Charlton took over the Picture Theatre at Lemington and it seems that his plans for Throckley were abandoned. The village had to await the opening of the Lyric in 1935 before it could boast a cinema again.

Marshall Rutter's old Picture Theatre in Tyne View, Lemington was taken over by John Grantham in July 1922, presumably as a temporary measure while he planned and built the Prince of Wales at the top end of Rokeby Street. After the latter cinema opened in July 1924, the Picture Theatre was run by Thomas Charlton. It then had one house each night with a mid-week programme change. Every Thursday night there was a 'go-as-you-please' (amateur variety).

Renewal of the licence was refused on 2 March 1927, possibly because the cinema was in poor condition; it certainly must have wilted from the competition offered by the Prince of Wales. On 30 March, Thomas Charlton submitted plans for the reconstruction of the cinema prepared by the Newcastle architects Cackett and Burns Dick. These called for a rebuild using the existing steel roof trusses, a stage with orchestra pit and two dressing rooms and seating for 398 on forms in the pit, 286 in the stalls and 216 in the balcony. The cinema, had it been built, would certainly have rivalled the Prince of Wales. The old building was burnt down about 1933 and the site was derelict until 1939, when air-raid shelters were built there. Part of a school now occupies the site.

The Prince of Wales had opened on 14 July 1924. The cinema's name was chosen as a result of a ballot in which 5,000 local people were said to have taken part. It was built for John Grantham. The cinema was on the stadium plan, with 534 seats in the stalls and 256 in the balcony, the two being separated by a barrier. There was a small stage and an orchestra pit. Below the stage were dressing rooms. The 'best of pictures' were to be supplemented by occasional weeks of variety and pantomimes.

'All the apartments are of an up-to-date character, and every precaution has been taken to guard against the danger of fire, both in the film rooms and in the hall itself. There are six exits, and in case of necessity, the whole building could be cleared in a minute.' The manager was J. Lambert

The Prince of Wales, Lemington, July 1924.

and the conductor of the orchestra Mr Robson. It was intended to have one performance nightly, except on Saturday when there would be two shows with, in addition, a children's matinée at 2.30 pm. Being outside the Newcastle boundary, there was a Sunday performance at 8 pm.

The cinema was opened by Major J.B. Rowell, chairman of Newburn UDC, who 'was convinced that picture houses had assisted in bringing about less drunkenness. He hoped the people of Lemington would flock to the house and in that way support Mr. Grantham in his good work.'

Throckley had been without a cinema since the destruction of the Imperial in 1922, but in the expansionist years of the mid-thirties and with a growing population in new housing estates, the time was right for change. The Hinge circuit built the Lyric in Newburn Road. The plans were for an 850-seat auditorium with a dance or assembly hall and seven lock-up shops. Although the design was basic for the period, with a minimum of ornamentation, the Lyric brought a new standard of luxury to cinema-going in the village.

It opened on 15 May 1935 with *The Thin Man* (William

The Lyric, Throckley, before 1963.

The auditorium of the Lyric, 1938.

Powell): the proceeds were donated to the Newburn and District Nursing Association, the Newburn Cottage Homes and other local charities. There were continuous shows every evening Monday to Saturday and one show on Sunday. Les Irwin recalled:

> … the building of a new cinema was looked forward to very eagerly. And when it finally materialised we were not disappointed. The interior was done out in the latest concept of cinema art, the seating was luxurious – and dou-ble-seating in the back row of the ninepennies was extremely popular and cosy for couples … [There was] a curtain which changed colours before the show started.
>
> [Mrs Sewell was also] … amazed at the ruched curtains which changed colour from orange to green to red. We who didn't actually live in Lemington changed our allegiance from the Prince of Wales to the Lyric. There was a young man dressed all in white with a white hat going around with ice cream. What bliss!'

In Newburn, the Imperial between the wars was recalled by Mr Finlay:

The outside was faced with vitrolite glass panels up to the canopy. The foyer was very cramped, with only a paybox and no confectionery kiosk. The cinema had an arrangement with a confectionery shop next door [Marchetti's] to supply sweets and ice cream during the interval … The show changed every Monday, Wednes-day and Friday, with [one show] on a Sunday.

Mrs Sewell recalled:

The Imperial, Newburn, c.1952.

The Newburn cinema was situated at the bottom of Station Road. It was small and not very plush inside. Downstairs the front stalls were more or less wooden benches; behind these were seats – not too comfortable. It was rather spartan but we didn't know anything else. … On a Saturday you had to book your seat: there were two houses, with a children's matinee in the afternoon. On a Sunday night there was one house, after the church came out. The films shown on a Sunday were rather old, but still the cinema was always full.

By 1936 the Imperial was feeling the pressure from the recently opened Lyric at Throckley, to which many patrons transferred their allegiance. It is possibly of this period that a client of the Grange Day Centre remembered: 'It was not thought a nice place to go.' In March 1936 the Imperial was taken over by Maurice Cohen (trading as Maurice Cinemas Ltd.). Performances were changed to continuous and seat prices raised.

In mid-1937 the Imperial began to advertise in the press

in a conscious effort to widen its appeal and there is a discernible improvement in the programming over the next few years from B-features to the occasional A. Often, the ritual mid-week change was varied by showing a weak film on Monday and Tuesday only with an A picture for the rest of the week. From 13 to 24 February 1939 the cinema was closed for 'extensive alterations'; seating was reduced to 550, presumably by the removal of the forms.

Mr Finlay remembered the Prince of Wales, Lemington, in the thirties:

The cinema had a change of programme on Monday and Thursday, and a one night show on Sunday. Though I never went to the Sunday show, I know they were very popular, as a lot of patrons came from the west end of Newcastle, as cinemas did not open there on Sunday. Later the programmes were changed Monday, Wednesday, Friday and Sunday. Sometimes if the film was a box-office winner it would be shown for six nights. … The cinema did employ some part-time staff who were not in uniform. I remember going one night at the back part of the week and it must have been the box office cashier's night off as the manager Mr Grantham issued me a ticket, then rushed out of the office to the circle entrance, halved my ticket, and showed me to the seat. He employed a bouncer with a loud voice to keep the kids quiet.

Once a year the local Amateur Operatic Society hired the cinema for a week to put on a stage show, which was usually Gilbert and Sullivan, sometimes other musical shows. All the advertising on the screen was with coloured slides, which seemed to be hand made; a few of the local shops took advantage of this medium. There were no trailers shown, only coloured slides showing the future attractions …'

Andy Forster recalled that there was a Saturday matinée at which seats were 1d, and that there was a vaudeville show on Thursday night, with singers, dancers, strongmen and local talent. Fruit, sweets and chocolate were available as refreshments.

The Lyric, Throckley was popular and was considered 'posh'; it outlasted most suburban cinemas, closing on 8 October 1966 and becoming a bingo club (bingo had gradually replaced films over several years). The manager thought that 'people would rather play bingo than go to a village cinema to see a film'. When local opposition prevented the owner from installing gaming machines in the mid-seventies, it was closed. It became a derelict and vandalised haven for glue-sniffers and others of a like mind. What remained of the building was demolished in May-June 1992.

When Samuel Piper of the Picture Palace, Westerhope, died in June 1927, the cinema was taken over by one of his sons, Robert, and later by Mary Ann Piper. In 1927 the balcony was enlarged and a small shop and rewind room added on the ground floor. Percy Longhorn, a cinema sound engineer, took over in 1932 and installed an Electrocord sound system (replaced by Mellophone in 1937). There were

Christopher Clavering

Mary Ann Piper, c.1929.

then live 'turns' at midpoint in the show.

From about 1938, Longhorn's son Leslie took over and with his wife ran the cinema until it closed. The Longhorns devoted their lives to their village cinema. When in 1941 Westerhope was cut off by snowstorms, films were brought from Newcastle by sledge. At about the same time the cinema was redecorated and it was decided that to celebrate this a new name should be chosen. A competition was run which produced the name 'Wavell' (for the British general then fighting in North Africa), but the name Orion was actually used.

The Orion survived when other cinemas fell to the challenge of television by cutting out the frills. Films were collected from Newcastle, not delivered. In addition to Mr and Mrs Longhorn, there were two full-time staff, usherettes-cum-cleaners. Mr Longhorn was his own projectionist.

The Orion, 1963.

The rest of the usherettes and helpers, including assistants on the job of decorating the cinema, are all volunteers. There are five or six youths and one girl who assist, and are totally unpaid except that they get free shows. We couldn't manage without them, especially on a Saturday or Sunday.

The Orion was shut down completely two weeks each year for Mr and Mrs Longhorn's holiday; it closed as a cinema in January 1970 and became a bingo club.

11 The rise of the multiplexes 1984-2005

In 1984 only four commercial cinemas remained in a city which had boasted 47, in city and suburbs, in 1939. In the city centre, the last survivors of the golden age of cinema-going in the thirties were the Haymarket, ABC (ex-Essoldo) and Odeon. In the suburbs, only the Jesmond remained. Cinema audiences nationally had fallen to an all-time low (at only three per cent of their 1947 total) but the multiplex cinema was just over the horizon; its arrival in Britain began a new chapter in the nation's cinema-going. First the decks had to be cleared of the remnants of a form of cinema-going which was rapidly becoming outmoded.

The Haymarket was the first to go. In the early 1950s the Haymarket site had been bought by King's College (later Newcastle University) and leased back to ABC; some of the leases were as short as three years. There was therefore no certain future for the cinema, which remained a single screen when the city's other large cinemas were being doubled or tripled. As insurance, ABC bought the Classic (former Essoldo) on Westgate Road in 1974; this became its main outlet in Newcastle.

The Haymarket was used for some extended runs in the 1970s, for example the locally filmed *Get Carter,* and *Superman,* but it was usually programmed concurrently with ABC1 in Sunderland; generally the newest films went to the former Essoldo. The usefulness of a large undivided auditorium was evident during the showing in 1980 of Abel Gance's

The Haymarket is demolished, 1985.

Newcastle Chronicle & Journal Ltd.

epic *Napoleon*, when the Northern Sinfonia Orchestra and a large audience were cheerfully accommodated. In May 1983 the Haymarket showed the 3-D version of *Friday the 13th, Part III*, and a bespectacled audience was seen in a cinema for the first time since the early fifties. Special lenses were fitted to the projectors and the spectacles were no longer red and green, but the show proved that there's no gimmick like an old one: one of the frighteners was a mouse on the end of a plank being thrust into the audience, first used by Audioscopiks in the 1930s.

In 1982 the beginning of the end was signalled when afternoon shows were abandoned. Thorn-EMI (formerly ABC) declined to renew the lease in September 1984. 'The amount of money involved in major refurbishment is quite substantial. We would really want more than three years' security of tenure'. The Haymarket closed on 20 September 1984. The cinema was demolished in January 1985, apart from the facade. The remains of the cinema were removed in 1987 and the resulting car park attractively landscaped.

At the Essoldo, the full stage facilities were used for probably the last time in the week beginning 7 December 1953, for the Latin-American revue *Braziliana*. In the mid-1950s, when Rank and Fox split over the installation of 4-track stereophonic sound in cinemas intended for Cinemascope, the Essoldo became a first run cinema for Fox films, some given two or three week runs. At the end of 1960 the cinema was reseated, redecorated and given a new screen installation prior to a long run of *Ben Hur*. At special prices (up to 10s 6d for a circle seat), this film ran for 21 weeks from 9 January 1961. The Essoldo then went back to routine programmes with the occasional extended run.

The Essoldo, 1966, showing the box lettering..

In October 1965 the organ was dismantled and the entire proscenium rebuilt to take a larger screen for 70mm presentations. The proscenium arch was replaced by sweep-round curtains. The organ lift was used to elevate a 'candy and coke bar'. Outside, the long 's's of Essoldo were replaced by new style box lettering. The cinema reopened on 27 January 1966 with *My Fair Lady*.

On 23 January 1971 the Essoldo closed for conversion to twin cinemas, the region's first. After work reported to have cost £170,000, the old stalls area (or most of it) became Essoldo 1, seating 650. Essoldo 2, seating 390, was created from the former circle. Both cinemas were equipped with 70mm facilities and six-track stereo. A licensed bar was added in 1972; in the same year the cinema was bought by Classic.

In March 1974 it was rumoured that EMI had approached Classic with an offer for the twins. The transfer was announced on 3 April. The two cinemas were to be renamed ABC 1 and 2. Behind EMI's interest was the problem with the group's main outlet in Newcastle, the Haymarket, the lease of which was under review. It was rumoured that EMI had paid well over the odds for the cinema as insurance against the lease of the Haymarket being suddenly terminated.

In 1986 the Thorn-EMI circuit was taken over by Cannon, beginning a period of uncertainty as the company, beset by financial problems, closed many of its cinemas. Added to this, Westgate Road was now something of a backwater, many of its buildings tatty and decaying. Alterations to the public transport system, particularly the downgrading of Marlborough Crescent bus station, had their effect. There was little car parking space in the vicinity and what there was, was not secure. On 18 September 1989 the cinema was offered for sale.

Two months later on 18 November, the closure of the Cannon was announced. Cannon management was clearly alarmed by the imminent opening of the Warner complex and was not willing to stay and fight for audiences. Ironically, the Newcastle Cannon had made an operating profit in its last year and had been refurbished. Business was reported to be back to the levels attained before the opening of the MetroCentre complex in Gateshead. The Cannon closed on 11 January 1990 and was demolished, the site becoming a car park. In 2004, an apartment block named Tyne Square was built there.

Since the war, the Odeon had been the city's premier cinema but by 1972 the vast 2,600-seat auditorium was seen as increasingly uneconomic. In October plans were revealed for its demolition and replacement with a seven-storey block containing shops on the basement, ground and first floor levels, with offices from the second to the seventh floors. Two cinemas, to seat 700 and 500 were to be squeezed into the first and second floors.

The problem for large auditoria like the Odeon's was explained by its manager, Fred Bower: 'What would be ideal would be a cinema with walls that opened and closed. I know that when I have Bond films, I wish it were the size of my last theatre, which had 4,000 seats.' The rebuilding plan was abandoned in favour of tripling the screens in the existing building. The Odeon closed on 25 January 1975, reopening on 9 March. Screen 1 was still large – by 1975 standards – with 1,228 seats. It was created from the circle; Screens 2 and 3, beneath the circle, were much smaller with 158 and 250 seats respectively. The whole complex was known as the Odeon Film Centre.

The next physical alteration to the Odeon was the addition of a fourth screen; this was located in the former stage area and part of the front stalls, and seated 361. Odeon 4 was officially opened on 1 February 1980 by the Lord Mayor; the film was a pre-release presentation of *Rocky II*. The new screen opened to the public on the following day with Breaking Away. The complex now had 1,997 seats, within reach of its original capacity as a single auditorium. Concessionary £1 admission to afternoon shows on Monday and Tuesday for the unemployed was introduced in May 1984. Student concessions followed. This year was later seen to have been the low point for cinema attendances nationally.

By 1987 the upward trend of admissions was evident: at the end of January *Crocodile Dundee* took over £28,000 in its first week at the Odeon, nearly £4,000 more than the cinema's best week in 1986. A new challenge in that year was the opening of the 10-screen AMC complex in Gateshead Metrocentre. The Odeon fought back successfully although it was later revealed that initially fifteen per cent of admissions were lost. A major refurbishment over two years cost £750,000 and included a licensed bar in the old upper rear circle foyer, the transfer of the paybox into the main foyer and the opening of a shop selling videos, magazines and confectionery. Odeon 1 was partially reseated with pullman seats, reducing capacity slightly to 1,171.

The arrival of the Warner Cinemas in December 1989 had no apparent effect on the Odeon. Manager Peter Talbot remarked: 'I'm expecting us to be as strong now as we have ever been. We may have only four screens, but that means we are able to play the four best films available – and in the real world, commercially there are only about four films out at any one time that people want to see.' Further redecoration and reseating took place in 1990. The Odeon continued

Neil Thompson

Odeon 1, the former circle, in 1985.

through the 1990s and into the new century, well-maintained and still popular.

In October 2000 it was listed Grade ll by the Department of Culture, Media and Sport on the recommendation of English Heritage. The Odeon was the 'only Paramount in England, and the only example of a mature Verity and Beverley cinema, to retain its original character inside and out. The transatlantic origins of this interior provide added interest'. The Odeon's horrified owners, Cinven, appealed against the listing, as it gave the building a measure of protection against demolition. The DCMS, at the first time of asking, immediately conceded that the Odeon had been wrongly listed by English Heritage, claiming that Ministers were not aware of the level of alteration to the building, and overturned the listing in June 2001.

The problem with the Odeon, at the time of writing, is that it forms part of a block which is ripe for redevelopment, much of which is owned by the developers, Multiplex. The city council then saw the retention of the Odeon as an obstacle to the redevelopment of this block and to its hopes of attracting a big-name department store, although it did envisage the possibility of the foyers being incorporated into any future development. A local group, led by the Northumberland and Newcastle Society, was established to promote the retention of the Odeon as a leisure space. With the opening of the new Odeon in the Gate development, the Pilgrim Street Odeon closed on 26 November 2002: the building awaits its fate.

A multiplex is usually defined as a cinema with five or more screens. They are often sited on the fringes of cities and towns where land is cheaper and cinemagoers are dependent on cars for accessing the cinema. The concept is, naturally, American and the first British multiplex opened in Milton Keynes in November 1985. The concept came to Tyneside on 14 October 1987 with the opening of the 2,470-seat, ten-screen AMC (now UCI) complex in the MetroCentre, Gateshead.

The first proposal for a multiplex in Newcastle was made in May 1988 as part of a leisure park scheme by local entrepreneur Joe Robertson. His chosen site was at Manors, east of the city centre but separated from it by a motorway. The northern part of the site had formerly been the North Eastern Railway's Manors Goods Station, destroyed by enemy action in 1941 and latterly used as a car park. It was on part of this 8-acre site that Robertson proposed a 16-screen cinema with car park. To the south across New Bridge Street, around Manors Metro Station, were to be a roller skating rink, a ten-pin bowl, an American diner and other facilities.

After a dispute concerning land ownership, by early June 1988 Robertson had disappeared from the scene and the cinema was to be built and operated by Warner Brothers, who proposed a 12-screen, 3,200-seat cinema. The city council sold the goods station site to Warners for a reported £1.25m and construction of the cinema began with a ground-breaking ceremony by actor Charles Dance on 14 February 1989.

As with the Paramount nearly sixty years before, an American company introduced the latest ideas in cinema design to the city. The main elevation, with its tall central atrium in metal and glass in the Warner Brothers colours of blue and yellow was a rather startling addition to the townscape. Within this was a large concourse containing the

CATS ticketing system and booking facilities. In the centre was a large concessions stand (probably where all the profit was made); on the left the Warner Brothers Studio Store and on the right a video games room.

The nine auditoria were to left and right from the rear of the concourse and were numbered clockwise from the left. The reduction in the number of screens from twelve to nine meant that some were larger than is normal in multi-screen complexes; total seating was 3386. When compared with the main concourse, the auditorium design was surprisingly traditional. The first impression was of height and space, unusual in a multiplex.

Sightlines from all seats were excellent; the larger auditoria each had a 'Cry Room' where fractious children could be taken out of the hearing of others while still able to see the film. For the hard of hearing, there was an infra-red transmission system using headsets. (Reminiscent of the thirties, when the Essoldo, Westgate and Queen's advertised their 'Ardente' deaf aids). Above the auditoria was a single long projection suite, serving all screens.

The total cost of the building was £4.5m.; there were 43 staff, of whom three were projectionists. After a formal ceremony on the morning of 6 December 1989 there was an open day; regular programmes began two days later. The poor quality of films then available resulted in lower than expected admissions in the first week, but these were reported to be well ahead of projected levels by February 1990. Children's Saturday matinées were introduced in January 1991.

However, the building's fairly remote location relative to the city centre remained a problem for the Warner (rebranded Warner Village in 1997) and around the end of the century

The Warner Brothers multiplex, 1990. It was to last fifteen years.

audiences declined, accelerated by the opening of the Odeon at the Gate in 2002. The cinema's accompanying food outlets closed and no other leisure facilities opened in the vicinity. In January 2004 the circuit's new owners, Vue Entertainment, admitted they were 'locked in talks with a mystery company which wants to buy the site'. The complex closed on 16 April 2004, the site having been bought by Northumbria University. The Warner was the shortest-lived of any major city cinema and was demolished in 2005.

The Gate is a huge £70m. leisure development of bars and restaurants, opened by Land Securities in 2002 on the site of the former Mayfair ballroom and offices in Newgate Street. One of the anchor tenants is the Odeon multiplex (replacing the Odeon in Pilgrim Street), which opened on the second floor on 27 November 2002 with a Gala Night. The official opening was by footballer Peter Beardsley; there was live match coverage in one of the screens, and a dragon display by members of the Chinese community. The new Odeon opened to the public on 28 November. With 12 screens and 2,569 seats, the new Odeon has Dolby SRD Digital Sound +; while screens 1,3,4 and 6 have Subtitling and Voice Description facilities for blind or partially sighted patrons. The screens are grouped into four large (the largest seating 436), four of medium size, and four small (the smallest seating 67). Approaching from the foyer along the tail of a 'Y', screens 1 and 2 are on the

The Odeon at the Gate, 2004.

left hand branch, screens 3 to 12 are in sequence along the right hand branch. Screens 1,3,4,9 and 10 have draw type curtains; the remainder reefer curtains. All have stadium seating and are decorated in muted reds and blues.

With the closure of the Warner Village, the Odeon has now a monopoly of the commercial cinema trade in the city. The Tyneside Cinema still offers a broad range of films, including many international titles. However, no other cinemas have been announced for the future, which is an indication of the decline of this once all-pervasive form of entertainment. Sixty years ago Newcastle had over 44,000 seats in 47 cinemas; today this figure has been reduced to less than 3,000 seats in two buildings.

12 Behind the scenes: the local film trade

In the very earliest days of the cinema films were sold direct to exhibitors by their makers at so much a foot. They were then sold on, second and third hand, to other exhibitors, the price and quality decreasing at each transaction. By about 1906 this practice was getting out of hand and certainly would not have been able to cope with the massive growth in the exhibiting side of the business from about 1908.

The first film exchange was established in America in 1903. An exchange bought films from their makers and rented them to exhibitors at about one quarter of their purchase price. Everyone in the business appeared to gain: makers had fewer but larger customers to buy their films at good prices; exhibitors had fewer but more comprehensive sources of product to show. The exchanges profited by keeping films on exhibition somewhere until their outlay had been recouped and a profit made.

By 1906 this system had been copied in Britain: in that year there were only four film exchanges, a number which grew to 242 (most of them small) by 1915. The new system spread through the country, based on regional centres outside London. In England and Wales, these were Birmingham, Cardiff, Leeds, Liverpool, Manchester and Newcastle. Newcastle was probably the smallest of the regional centres, responsible for distribution in what used to be called the 'Four Northern Counties' of Northumberland, Durham, Cumberland and Westmorland, an area in which, in 1926, there were thought to be about 200 cinemas, rising by 1951 to 370.

The first renter in Newcastle was Henderson's North of England Film Bureau, founded in 1906. The peak year was 1926 when there were 27 renting firms in the city. Initially these were all locally based, but these small enterprises were almost all taken over or supplanted by branches of London-based firms. From the 1920s the local renters declined (only Henderson's were still trading by the mid-1930s; they hung

Apex films was a renter with premises in Westgate Road.

Frank Manders

on until about 1950), to be replaced by gradual domination of the big British and US production companies.

As the number of cinemas declined in the 1960s, the number of distributors did likewise and many of the Hollywood majors no longer felt it necessary to maintain offices in the English regions. By 1968 Rank was the only UK company to have a Newcastle office, though seven US companies still did. The final decline was abrupt: by 1971 only Disney still had a Newcastle office, the rest employed individuals working from private addresses.

As in London, where the film business grouped together initially in Cecil Court off Charing Cross Road and later in Wardour Street, so in Newcastle, the Bigg Market and Pudding Chare initially found favour, to be supplanted within a few years by Westgate Road. The attraction of Westgate Road was possibly the large amount of relatively inexpensive office space in the area, which was at the margin of the main business and commercial area but still convenient for the central railway station. The renters were certainly all grouped together in Westgate Road by 1914, when seven of the nine renters had their offices there, and the remaining two were not far away. Once this nucleus had been established, newcomers joined it: 22 of the 26 were in Westgate Road or adja-

The Stoll cinema café, 1933.

cent streets in 1925. They were joined there in the 1930s by the offices of local cinemas and cinema circuits, equipment suppliers, etc., so that the Westgate Road-Bath Lane area was like a film colony.

The renters were a gregarious bunch. In the 1930s they and the exhibitors with offices in the area worked in their offices in the morning, met for lunch in the Stoll cinema café, then adjourned to a nearby pub, usually the Brandy Vaults (now Tilley's), where more business was done, then either went back to their offices or staggered off home. Renters and exhibitors ran a local trade magazine called *Northern Lights* briefly in 1919-20 and they played football, snooker and golf against each other. They raised money to endow a cot in the Children's Hospital. There were trade dances.

The objective of the renters was to get the rights to the very best films from the production companies and to book then into as many cinemas in the area as they possibly could. Before the First World War, according to an article in the *Kinematograph Weekly*, the renters had it all their own way, with exhibitors queuing at their offices for product, but during and after the war, with the numbers of renters increasing, the positions were reversed. Renters fought back with what were called 'exclusives' and block booking.

All the renters employed salesmen who went from cinema to cinema selling the company's product, and organised trade shows of new films. These trade shows were usually held at one of four cinemas in Newcastle: the Pavilion, Stoll, Queen's Hall and Westgate. (All these except the Queen's were conveniently in Westgate Road). The renters demanded optimum conditions for their shows and these cinemas tended to have the best projection and music, which benefited ordinary cinemagoers. Most trade shows took place at 10.30 or 11.00 in the morning before the cinema opened to the public. By the period of the First World War, the major renting companies like Jury and Fox were also incorporating small theatres, seating 15-30, in their own offices so that trade shows could be given at any time of the day.

The other main responsibilities of the renters were distribution of films to cinemas and the storage and running maintenance of the films themselves between engagements. Films for cinemas in 'country' areas were sent by rail or (later) by Film Transport Services. Those for city cinemas were normally collected from renters' offices by junior projectionists or rewind lads (owners thereby saving money).

Douglas Gibson, while working at the Plaza in 1940,

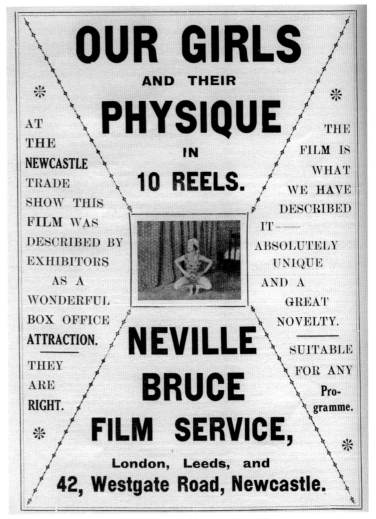

Northern Lights, 1919, advertises an enticing film!

recalled that 'we had to go down town to collect the films twice a week. MGM offices and film depot were in Westgate Road along with Twentieth Century Fox, and further down opposite the Pavilion GFD [General Film Distributors] and Universal. Warner Bros. offices were almost opposite the Essoldo with United Artists and Columbia in the same building, but their film stores were all in Heron's Yard at the lower end of Corporation Street. We used an old kitbag to carry the feature films and shorts in their battered and rusting tin boxes.' The Essoldo was so convenient that films were carried across Westgate Road in a wheelbarrow.

As an example of these businesses, the Twentieth Century Fox office in Newcastle just before the second World War employed about 25 people. There was the office manager and his clerical staff, a chief salesman with four staff, four women who worked in the film repair department at the back of the building, and two lads, known as the 'the barrow boys', who transported cans of film to the Central station for despatch. There were two salesmen's offices and a 'synopsis' room which, in addition to synopses of films currently on release, contained posters and cardboard cut-outs for foyer displays.

Lesser companies had much smaller establishments, many gathered together in Heron's Yard, off Corporation Street (in the premises occupied by Norland Cables in 2005). This development seems to have come about because of the Cross House fire of 23 December 1919. Cross House was (and is) a six-storey office block, completed in 1912. In 1919 part of the basement was occupied by Famous Lasky's offices and film storage vaults. A fire began there, possibly caused by an electrical fault setting fire to films (the inquest never made mat-

The Twentieth Century Fox offices on Westgate Road, 1942.

ters totally clear) and shot up the stairs and lift-shaft. Twelve people were killed, some by jumping from the roof. All sorts of horrors were revealed – the lift shaft and the stairs which wound round it were the only means of exit and the city's fire brigade did not possess a turntable ladder long enough to reach the roof. The film trade was blamed.

The city adopted new regulations for film storage (based on those of the LCC) and G.W. Heron began building film stores for rent on land behind a mineral water factory on Corporation Street, which already was occupied by some wooden(!) sheds used for film storage. New brick stores were built in 1923 'in accordance with the Celluloid and Cinematograph Films Act of 1922' (another result of the Cross House tragedy). The buildings were gradually added to from 1927 to 1949, when they reached their greatest extent. On the ground floor of each unit were the film vaults and despatch counter, while on the first floor were repair rooms and empty film tin stores.

In the cinema's earliest years before the First World War, most halls were small and tended to be owned and run as family businesses. Even then, however, the more forward-looking owners saw the advantages of forming a group of cinemas, or circuit, under their control. The gains were mainly economic: a circuit gave greater power in the eternal struggle against renters and distributors; staff and films could be exchanged between cinemas; while profits from small halls could be used to expand the circuit with larger and, it was hoped, more profitable cinemas.

The first major circuit formed in the north-east was built up by the Black family of Sunderland. George Black I (1858-1910) opened the former Bonnersfield Presbyterian Chapel as

The disastrous Cross House fire of 1919 which started in Famous Lasky's offices in the basement.

the Monkwearmouth Picture Hall in May 1906; from this modest beginning the Black circuit expanded rapidly under George Black II (1891-1945) who took over at the age of 19. After creating picture halls from failing variety theatres across the north-east from 1908, the circuit's first venue in Newcastle was the Byker Grand, acquired in 1913. Also in

1913, George Black II became a partner in City Varieties Co., Ltd., which ran the Pavilion in Westgate Road. In 1919, possibly to finance a boxing stadium in Sunderland, the Black circuit (then down to seven cinemas from a peak of 13) was sold to J.G. Thompson and A. Collins for a reported £200,000. Thompson and Collins (a brother of Joseph Collins and managing director of the Grainger Picture House) added the Pavilion to the circuit before selling their cinemas in 1928 to Denman Picture Houses, a Gaumont-British subsidiary. Meanwhile, George Black II had built up a new circuit based on Newcastle and comprising (among others) the Queen's Hall, the Grainger, the Grey Street, the Scala, Heaton, and the Globe, Gosforth. These cinemas became part of the General Theatres Corporation, which George II joined as a founding director in 1928. GTC was itself taken over by Gaumont-British later in the year and this circuit gained a strong presence in Newcastle.

Sidney Bacon (1878-1927) was a Newcastle theatre manager who, by 1904, was managing the Grand, Byker, the Olympia, Newcastle and the Metropole, Gateshead; he was also joint lessee, with Richard Thornton, of Olympia. He left Newcastle to enter the cinema business in London and began to build a nation-wide circuit. In Newcastle he took over the new Olympia in 1910 and the Star in 1911. But his circuit expanded away from Newcastle, in Carlisle, York, London and the south coast. By 1919 there

Thomas France, c.1929.

were seven cinemas, by 1930 there were 31. The circuit was based in London and was run after Bacon's death by Thomas France. All the former Bacon halls went to Union Cinemas in 1936.

Other circuits were more local in scope. The largest of these was founded by Stanley Rogers (1858-1933). Although his obituary states that he 'came to Tyneside shortly after the end of the Great War', he is to be found man-

Stanley Rogers, c.1929.

aging the Empire, Blaydon, in 1914. With E.J. (Teddy) Hinge as general manager, Stanley Rogers Cinemas expanded rapidly in the 1920s, both in the north-east and on the Cumbrian coast. The company acquired small, run-down halls and by careful management restored them to profitability. In Newcastle, examples were the Gaiety and the Palladium. Rogers died in October 1933, shortly before the completion of what was probably the first cinema to be built by the company as new, the Regal, Fenham.

The company (actually an interlocking network of companies) was then run by Teddy Hinge (1888-

Teddy Hinge, c.1929.

1961), eventually becoming Hinge Circuit Cinemas. In the thirties, income from the smaller cinemas was used to build several medium-sized but attractive new halls, usually in partnership with others. In Newcastle, these were the Royalty, Gosforth, the Lyric, Throckley and the Rialto, Benwell. At the same time, older cinemas were added to the circuit: the Grand, Benwell, the Globe, Gosforth and the Grand Theatre, Byker. By the end of the decade, there were 15 cinemas and theatres in the circuit.

The business was run, as were all small circuits, with extreme care. One of Hinge's projectionists remembered:

… all stores had to be used extremely sparingly to save cash. Carbons used in the arc lamps had to be used till they were a mere two-and-a-half inches short as stubs: we were supplied with metal holders to enable this saving to be carried out. All light bulbs had to be accounted for when replaced or your supply was not renewed … We were even encouraged to clean the bayonet caps with metal polish to make them look brand new and not used. These were collected from time to time and sent back to Crompton Parkinson Ltd as duds and refunds claimed.

Like many cinema pioneers, Teddy Hinge had begun his show business career as an actor; the theatre remained his first love. Profits from the cinema circuit were poured into two 'dying theatres', the Grand, Byker and the Hippodrome, Darlington, in a vain attempt to keep variety alive. What remained of the cinema circuit was dismantled in the early 1960s.

James MacHarg was a Wallsend builder whose first venture into cinema ownership was in his home town with the Tyne and the Royal. His first and for many years his only cinema in Newcastle was the Brinkburn, Byker. In 1923 he formed a new company, Tyne Picture Houses Ltd., with a capital of £10,000. This company built the super-cinema, the Apollo, in 1933. A further group of cinemas was managed but not wholly owned by MacHarg. These were the Lyric,

James MacHarg, c.1929.

Heaton, the Jesmond and the Grainger in Newcastle, along with the Shipcote, Gateshead, the Lyric, Howdon and the Howard Hall, North Shields. All the cinemas were however run as a circuit, with interchange of relief staff and all films centrally booked. By 1961 only the Apollo and the Jesmond remained and these were sold to Arnold Sheckman in 1963-64.

A circuit of around eleven cinemas, all of them small halls, was that run by Sydney Dawe and J.H. Dawe as DB (Dawe Brothers) Cinemas. Although based in Newcastle, the brothers had only one cinema in the city, the Imperial, Byker. Other cinemas in the circuit at various times were the Apollo and the Theatre Royal, Birtley, the Rex and the Theatre Royal, Hebburn, the Empire and the Theatre Royal, Jarrow, the

Sydney Dawe, c.1929.

Empress and the Palladium, Gateshead, the Regal, Wheatley Hill, the Palace, Wingate and the Hippodrome, Thornley. Later the Carlton, Tynemouth was added. Most of these cinemas were converted to bingo halls. Linked to DB Cinemas was DRC Cinemas, the 'R' being Leslie Renwick of the Bamborough and the 'C' Carter Crowe.

Like James MacHarg, H.T. and W.A. Smelt, who later traded as Northern Cinemas, were builders. Their first involvement with the cinema was with the King's, Annfield Plain in 1912. The circuit owned three cinemas in Chester-le-Street in the late 1930s. In Newcastle they owned the Plaza, the Savoy and the Rex. The circuit was broken up in about 1953, most of the cinemas going to Essoldo, although the Plaza and the Rex were taken over by W.J. Clavering.

Joseph Broughton, c.1929.

Almost too small to be considered a circuit were the six cinemas owned by Joseph Broughton and William R. Marshall. In Newcastle they owned the Stanhope Grand and the Raby Grand. Elsewhere were the Picture House, Forest Hall, the Queen's, Wallsend, the Crown, Tyne Dock and George Black's old hall at Monkwearmouth, which they named the Bromarsh after themselves.

William R. Marshall, c.1929

The third largest cinema circuit in the country, Essoldo, was based in Newcastle. Owning 196 cinemas at its peak, this empire was latterly run from offices in City Chambers, Grey Street, although there was a London office responsible for film booking. Sol Sheckman (1891-1963) was said to have bought his first cinema, the Gaiety in Sunderland, when he left school at 15. This would have been in 1906, but unfortunately for this story, the Gaiety did not open until 1913. Sheckman began as a boxing promoter in Blyth in the mid-twenties, moving on to St James's Hall, Newcastle. His cinema career seems to have begun in November 1923 with ownership of the Victory, Crawcrook. In February 1924 he formed North-Eastern Theatres Ltd., (later North East Coast Cinemas, Ltd.,) which ran the Hippodrome, Crook, the Co-op Hall and the Palace High Spen, and the Empire, Tudhoe.

He founded a second company, S.S. Blyth Kinemas Ltd. in August 1931, which began with the former Black Brothers' Theatre Royal, Blyth. Both circuits expanded and were merged into Essoldo (also formed in 1931), a name derived from the first names of his wife Esther, himself, and his daughter, Dorothy. Essoldo cinemas were broadly of two types, the large modern super-cinema (like the Essoldo, Newcastle) and the smaller, older halls which were acquired cheaply and given the benefits of a large circuit. In Newcastle, examples of the latter were the Crown, Savoy and Scala. In the sixties many of the small cinemas were closed or turned over to bingo; the flagship Newcastle Essoldo was sold to Classic in 1972.

The struggle for Sunday opening

All picture halls were licensed under the Cinematograph Act of 1909; in Newcastle the Town Improvement and Watch Committees of the city council were responsible for regulation of cinemas in the city. The most important rules were concerned with public safety, but most local authorities were unable to resist the temptation to regulate the content of films and when they could be shown. In the years up to the First World War the question of whether or not going to the pictures on a Sunday should be allowed was a matter of constant debate throughout the country. Where it was allowed, all proceeds were given to charity. From 1912 Newcastle authorities were steadfastly opposed to Sunday opening, although some neighbouring local authorities were more liberal. In Newcastle, it was felt that Sunday should be special and that the working classes should not be robbed of their day of rest. The chief opponents of Sunday opening were the churches, often supported by the trade unions.

During the First World War, most picture halls had promoted concerts in aid of the war effort and had given over their stages to official speakers. Supported by workmen from Elswick and Scotswood, it was suggested that four of the city's picture halls should open on Sundays on a rota basis, with proceeds going to the Lord Mayor's War Relief Fund, but the vote on 1 May 1918 was lost 28-25.

The Sunday Entertainments Act of 1932 permitted the opening of cinemas on Sunday after a vote of townspeople. Deputations asked the city council to defend what was left of the British Sunday: 'What with hiking, biking, all the year round wireless services, facilities by motor car and train, and now the proposal to cut the jugular vein of the Churches…'. There were also objections from some of the owners of smaller cinemas, who would have to employ additional projectionists for Sunday opening. It was felt that all the pressure was coming from the larger circuit cinemas, with the local CEA in favour of opening. People who wanted to see a film on a Sunday had to travel out of the city, usually to Gateshead, Gosforth, Forest Hall or Wallsend: in the course of a debate in April 1933, one city councillor confessed that 'he was able to take his family in the car to Morpeth and enjoy a cinema there'; it is likely that few of his electors had this facility. In the late 1930s the Saturday *Evening Chronicle* helpfully provided listings of Sunday films at cinemas in neighbouring areas.

The question was not raised again until 1949, by which time, it was claimed, Newcastle was the only city of any size without Sunday opening. At a time of mounting concern about juvenile delinquency, there was determined opposition to change from an array of free church groups, opposition which was unlikely to be outweighed by support of the city branch of the Young

Communist League. The cinema industry itself continued to encompass opposing opinions on the matter. A letter from the local CEA in 1952 revealed that the Welbeck, Vaudeville, Bamboro, Imperial, Heaton Electric, Embassy, Rex, Plaza, Stoll, Gem, Regent and Brighton, all independent, opposed opening because of 'hooliganism and damage done by Sunday night audiences [elsewhere] and also the poor quality films available … from the Renters'. In favour of opening were the managements of three ABC cinemas, four Rank, four Essoldo, three MacHarg, the Gloria, the Raby and Black's Regal. After debating the issue on four occasions in four years, the council agreed at last to leave it to the public to vote on the matter.

A poll of electors was held on 30 October 1952 which resulted in twice as many people voting in favour of Sunday opening as were opposed (although the low poll of only 20 per cent of the electorate allowed the churches to claim a moral victory). Licences were issued to 24 cinemas on 10 April 1953 (12 did not bother to apply) and the new dispensation began on 19 April. When the people finally achieved what they had voted for, they found that because of the problems of film transport between cities, shorter opening hours and lower box office takings, what they were offered was cheaper ancient films, often five or six years old. The local press noted that at around 10 pm on the first Sunday 'Some cinema halls were two thirds empty'. Only the Haymarket thought to start its week on Sunday rather than Monday with an up-to-date film and reaped the reward of a full house. The other city centre cinemas soon followed suit. The Sunday band concerts at the Odeon, Essoldo and Westgate were abandoned. The arrival of Sunday opening was something of a hollow victory for its supporters, as the decline of traditional cinema-going was beginning.

30,000 ATTEND FIRST NIGHT OF SUNDAY CINEMAS

Queues start an hour before opening

MORE than 30,000 people attended the 24 cinemas in Newcastle which opened for Sunday films last night.

Some queues formed as early as 4.30 p.m. for performances at six o'clock, and there was again a constant flow of patrons for the second showing which ended at 10.30.

A notable feature, the "Journal" was told, was the absence of the hooliganism which has marked some of the Sunday concerts held in cinemas in the city centre.

Newcastle Journal reports on the success of the first Sunday opening.

The coming of sound

Cinema	date	film	sound system
Stoll	11 May 1929	*The Singing Fool*	WE
Queen's Hall	24 June 1929	*Show Boat*	WE
Adelaide	14 October 1929	*Broadway Melody*	WE
Palladium	18 November 1929	*Movietone Follies*	BTP
New Westgate	25 November 1929	*King of the Khyber Rifles*	RCA
Olympia	25 November 1929	*Broadway Melody*	WE
Heaton	9 December 1929	*Movietone Follies*	WE
Grainger	30 December 1929	*White Cargo*	RCA
Bamboro'	20 January 1930	*Broadway Melody*	WE
Brighton	20 January 1930	*Broadway Melody*	WE
Welbeck	20 January 1930	*The Singing Fool*	RCA
Empire	3 February 1930	*The Informer*	RCA
Plaza	10 February 1930	*Lucky in Love*	BA
Pavilion	10 February 1930	*Pleasure Crazed*	RCA
Grand Theatre	14 April 1930	*Honky Tonk*	BTP
Globe	28 April 1930	*Sunny Side Up*	BA
Scala	28 April 1930	*The Street Girl*	BA
Grey Street	28 July 1930	*His Glorious Night*	BA
Majestic	4 August 1930	*Men Without Women*	WE
Gaiety	8 September 1930	*High Society Blues*	BTP
Brinkburn	20 September 1930	*Cohens & Kellys*	BTP
Jesmond	10 November 1930	*Sunny Side Up*	WE
King's Hall	17 November 1930	*Hearts in Exile*	Electrocord

In addition, the following cinemas had sound by the end of 1930: Grand (Cinephone); Prince of Wales (Cinephone) and Raby (Edibell).

WE - Western Electric; RCA - Radio Corporation of America; BTP - British Talking Pictures; BA - British Acoustic; BTH - British Thompson-Houston.

Newcastle cinema organs

Cinema	organ type	opened	fate
Black's Regal	Compton 3c/6	1934	Majorca, 1969
Empire	Unknown *('of considerable power')*	1913	Unknown
Essoldo	Lafleur *(Hammond) electronic*	1938	Private, 1965
(New) Pavilion	Nicholson and Lord *2m. straight/15 speaking stops*	1919	Removed
New Westgate	WurliTzer 2/6	1930	Scrapped for spares, 1959
Paramount	WurliTzer 2/19	1931	Removed 1964; for sale (2004)
Plaza	Blackett and Howden *2m. straight/18 speaking stops*	1928	Removed
Queen's Hall	Vincent *3m. straight/ 29 speaking stops*	1920	Removed 1955
Scala	Vincent 2m straight	?	Unknown
Stoll	Nicholson and Lord *2m. straight/11 speaking stops**	1919	Removed 1942

* rebuilt by Blackett & Howden 1928

Jimmy Swift at the Paramount's WurliTzer c.1935

Thirteen weeks or more
notable extended runs in Newcastle

Film	cinema	start date	run
The Sound of Music	Queen's Hall	18 Apr 1965	140 weeks
South Pacific	Queen's Hall	22 Sept 1958	81 weeks
Love Story	Essoldo	23 July 1971	29$\frac{1}{2}$ weeks+
How the West was Won	Queen's Hall	3 Nov 1963	29 weeks
Where Eagles Dare	Queen's Hall	20 July 1969	29 weeks*
Lawrence of Arabia	Queen's Hall	7 Apr 1963	26 weeks**
Close Encounters of the Third Kind	Queen's Hall	27 Mar 1978	26 weeks
The Guns of Navarone	Queen's Hall	14 May 1961	22 weeks
Paint Your Wagon	Essoldo	13 Apr 1970	22 weeks
A Star is Born	ABC 1 & 2	8 May 1977	22 weeks
Ben Hur	Essoldo	9 Jan 1961	21 weeks
West Side Story	Queen's Hall	27 May 1962	20 weeks
Ryan's Daughter	Queen's Hall	4 July 1971	21 weeks
ET	Haymarket	5 Dec 1982	21 weeks%
Oliver	Pavilion	22 Dec 1968	18 weeks
Song of Norway	Queen's Hall	27 Dec 1970	18 weeks
Genevieve (re-run)	Grainger	12 Jan 1953	17 weeks
Can Can	Queen's Hall	6 June 1960	17 weeks
Cleopatra	Pavilion	19 Jan 1964	17 weeks
My Fair Lady	Essoldo	27 Jan 1966	17 weeks
Doctor Zhivago	Essoldo	6 Oct 1966	17 weeks
A Man for All Seasons	Pavilion	14 May 1967	17 weeks
Gone With the Wind (reissue)	Essoldo	7 Nov 1968	17 weeks
Funny Girl	Queen's Hall	30 April 1969	16 weeks
Gandhi	Odeon 4,3,2	17 Feb 1983	16 weeks
The Quiet Man (re-run)	Grainger	31 Aug 1953	15 weeks
Hello Dolly	Queen's Hall	10 May 1970	15 weeks
Fiddler on the Roof	Queen's Hall	20 Feb 1972	15 weeks
Return of the Jedi	Odeon 1,2,3,4	2 June 1983	14 weeks
55 Days at Peking	Pavilion	13 Oct 1962	14 weeks
The Empire Strikes Back	Odeon	15 June 1980	14 weeks++
The Ten Commandments	Queen's Hall	26 May 1958	13 weeks
Around the World in 80 Days	Queen's Hall	23 Dec 1957	13 weeks
Wonderful World of the Brothers Grimm	Queen's Hall	28 June 1964	13 weeks
Jaws	Haymarket	21 Dec 1974	13 weeks
The Great Waltz	Queen's Hall	28 Jan 1973	13 weeks
Lost Horizon	Queen's Hall	6 May 1972	13 weeks
The Longest Day	Queen's Hall	23 Dec 1962	13 weeks

+6$\frac{1}{2}$ weeks at Screen 1, immediately followed by 23 weeks at Screen 2.

*20 weeks at the Queen's Hall, immediately followed by 7 weeks at the Pavilion.

**6 weeks at the Queen's Hall, immediately followed by 20 weeks at the Pavilion.

% 7 weeks at the Haymarket, 4 weeks at ABC 1, 10 weeks at ABC 2.

++ 12 weeks at Odeon 1, immediately followed by 2 weeks at Odeon 4.

Directory (cinemas' original names)

Cinema: Adelaide
Address: Adelaide Tce/Maria St, Benwell
Architect: Charles S Errington, Ncle
Builder: William Jackson, Ncle
Decorator: Unknown
Capacity: 640 (504 stalls, 136 balcony)
Opens: 17 October 1910
Closes: 1 February 1943
Present use: Autoparts shop

Cinema: Apollo (1)
Address: Shields Road, Byker
Architect: Pascal J Stienlet, Ncle
Builder: Davison, Eason, Harkness, Ncl
Decorator: R J Richardson, Ncle
Capacity: 1,650 in stalls and circle
Opens: 28 December 1933
Closes: 6 May 1941 (bombed)
Present use: see Apollo (2)

Cinema: Apollo (2) (rebuild Apollo (1))
Address: Shields Road, Byker
Architect: Pascal J Stienlet & Son Ncle
Builder: Stanley Miller Ltd., Ncle
Decorator: M Alexander & Sons., Ncle
Capacity: 576 (936 stalls, 640 circle)
Opens: 19 March 1956
Closes: 1 October 1983
Present use: Demolished

Cinema: Bamborough
Address: Union Road, Byker
Architect: Newcombe & Newcombe, Ncle
Builder: Unknown
Decorator: Unknown
Capacity: 750 (500 stalls, 250 circle)
Opens: ?16 July, 1913
Closes: 11 April 1959
Present use: Demolished

Cinema: Black's Regal (later Odeon)
Address: Shields Road, Byker
Architect: Edwin M Lawson, Ncle
Builder: Henry Waller, Ncle
Decorator: Unknown
Capacity: 1,645 (1,120 stalls, 525 circle)
Opens: 3 September 1934
Closes: 11 November 1972
Present use: Demolished

Cinema: Brighton
Address: Westgate Road/Lynnwood Terrace
Architect: Marshall & Tweedy, Ncle
Builder: James McEwen, Ncle
Decorator: Unknown
Capacity: 1,085 (767 stalls, 318 circle)
Opens: 10 July 1911
Closes: 20 April 1963
Present use: 10-pin bowling alley

Cinema: Brinkburn
Address: 14 Brinkburn Street, Byker
Architect: J Newton Fatkin, Ncle
Builder: Unknown
Decorator: Unknown
Capacity: 922 (657 stalls, 265 circle)
Opens: 25 February 1910
Closes: 2 July 1960
Present use: Demolished

Cinema: Crown
Address: 818-830 Scotswood Road
Architect: White and Stephenson, Ncle
Builder: W T Weir, Howdon
Decorator: W Ferguson & Son, Ncle (plaster)
Capacity: 1041 (465 stalls, 387 pit, 189 circle)
Opens: 24 December 1910
Closes: 24 November 1962
Present use: Demolished, 1971

Cinema: Electra
Address: Denton Road, Scotswood
Architect: William Glover, Ncle (original)
Builder: Unknown
Decorator: Unknown
Capacity: Unknown
Opens: by 8 December 1910
Closes: circa 12 January 1911
Present use: Demolished

Cinema: Elswick
Address: 818-830 Scotswood Road
Architect: Charles S Errington, Ncle (original)
Builder: Unknown
Decorator: Unknown
Capacity: 1,200 (estimated)
Opens: before 9 November 1908
Closes: 16 January 1909
Present use: Demolished, 1909-10

Cinema: Embassy
Address: Thorntree Drive, Denton
Architect: Robert Burke, Ncle
Builder: J W Longstaff & J Bain, Ncle
Decorator: Fred A Foster, Nottingham
Capacity: 988 (626 stalls, 362 circle; stadium)
Opens: 6 September 1937
Closes: 25 June 1960
Present use: Bingo club

Cinema: Empire
Address: 10-12 Grainger Street West
Architect: W & T R Milburn, Sunderland
Builder: Stephen Easten Ltd., Ncle
Decorator: F de Jong, London
Capacity: 614 (456 stalls, 158 circle)
Opens: 2 April 1913
Closes: 11 November 1933
Present use: Demolished

Cinema: Essoldo (Classic, ABC, EMI, Cannon)
Address: Westgate Road/Thornton Street
Architect: William Stockdale, North Shields
Builder: Hastie Burton, North Shields
Decorator: M Alexander & Son, Ncle
Capacity: 2109 (1144 stalls, 965 circle)
Opens: 29 August 1938
Closes: 11 January 1990
Present use: Demolished

Cinema: Gaiety
Address: 12 Nelson Street
Architect: Percy L Browne, Ncle (conversion)
Builder: Unknown
Decorator: Unknown
Capacity: 875 (550 stalls, 325 circle)
Opens: 29 March 1911 (but see text)
Closes: 26 February 1949
Present use: Demolished (facade remains)

Cinema: Gem
Address: 115 Elswick Road
Architect: Barnes & Burton, Ncle (cversion)
Builder: Unknown
Decorator: Unknown
Capacity: 350
Opens: 6 April 1911
Closes: c.1912 (exact date unknown)
Present use: Demolished

Cinema: Gem
Address: Tindal Street
Architect: Edwin M Lawson, Chester-le-Street
(for conversion)
Builder: Unknown
Decorator: Unknown
Capacity: 630
Opens: 8 January 1934
Closes: 29 August 1960
Present use: Demolished

Cinema: Globe
Address: Salters Road, Gosforth
Architect: J J Hill, Ncle
Builder: John Jackson & Son, Ncle
Decorator: Unknown
Capacity: 883
Opens: 19 December 1910
Closes: 25 November 1961
Present use: Restaurant and shops

Cinema: Gloria
Address: St Anthony's Road, Walker
Architect: Albert Fennel, Gateshead
Builder: Gordon. Durham & Co., E Boldon
Decorator: Webster Davidson & Co., S'land
Capacity: 1184 (762 stalls, 422 balcony)
Opens: 11 April 1938
Closes: 4 March 1962
Present use: Demolished

Cinema: Grainger (1)
Address: 26-28 Grainger Street
Architect: Percy L Browne and Glover, Ncle
Builder: Unknown
Decorator: Unknown
Capacity: 775 (566 stalls, 209 circle)
Opens: 1 December 1913
Closes: 31 July 1937
Present use: See Grainger (2)

Cinema: Grainger (2)
Address: 26-28 Grainger Street
Architect: Marshall and Tweedy, Ncle
Builder: W W Kelsey, Ncle
Decorator: R W Smiles, Ncle (plasterwk)
Capacity: 733 (515 stalls, 218 circle)
Opens: 2 December 1937
Closes: 26 March 1960
Present use: Demolished (shops)

Cinema: Grand
Address: 3 Condercum Road, Benwell
Architect: Gibson and Stienlet, North Shields
Builder: Unknown
Decorator: Anderson's, S. Shields (plasterwk)
Capacity: 666 (448 stalls, 192 circle, 26 boxes)
Opens: 7 August 1911
Closes: 26 September 1956
Present use: Demolished

Cinema: Grand Theatre
Address: Wilfred Street, Byker
Architect: William Hope, Ncle
Builder: S F Davidson, Heaton
Decorator: Dean, Birmingham
Capacity: 1272
Opens: 27 July 1896
Closes: 27 August 1954
Present use: Demolished

Cinema: Haymarket
Address: Percy Street/Haymarket Lane
Architect: George Bell (Dixon and Bell), Ncle
Builder: Thomas Clements & Son., Ncle
Decorator: M Alexander & Son., Ncle
Capacity: 1,280 (902 stalls, 378 circle); 2,002
(1,296 stalls, 706 circle) after 1936.
Opens: 21 December 1933
Closes: 20 September 1984
Present use: Demolished

Cinema: Heaton
Address: North View, Heaton
Architect: White and Stephenson, Ncle
Builder: William Thompson, Ncle
Decorator: Ferguson & Co., Ncle
Capacity: 825 (390 stalls, 223 pit, 312 circle)
Opens: 21 November 1910
Closes: 17 June 1961
Present use: Bingo club

Cinema: Hippodrome (Ginnett's Circus)
Address: Northumberland Road
Architect: Thomas V Woodhouse, Nott'm
Builder: Thomas V Woodhouse, Nott'm
Decorator: Mortimer Bros., York
Capacity: ?2,000
Opens: 18 May 1908; 1 March 1909
Closes: 18 June 1908; ?16 March 1909
Present use: Demolished, 1909

Cinema: Imperial
Address: Station Road, Newburn
Architect: Thomas R Eltringham, Throckley
Builder: Unknown
Decorator: Unknown
Capacity: 550 initially, 720 in 1913
Opens: 18 October 1911 (licensing date)
Closes: ?13 May 1961
Present use: Offices

Cinema: Imperial (later Stanhope Grand)
Address: Worley Street/corner Longley Street
Architect: Austin & Johnson, Ncle (original)
Builder: Unknown
Decorator: Unknown
Capacity: 604 (520 stalls, 84 circle)
Opens: 10 August 1908
Closes: (dance hall, 5 January 1932)
Present use: Demolished

Cinema: Jesmond
Address: Lyndhurst Avenue, West Jesmond
Architect: White and Stephenson, Ncle
Builder: ?William Thompson, Heaton
Decorator: Unknown
Capacity: 998 (486 stalls, 269 pit, 243 circle)
Opens: 2 May 1921
Closes: 1 October 1993
Present use: Unknown (building standing)

Cinema: King's Hall
Address: Marlborough Crescent
Architect: James E Parsons, Ncle (original)
Builder: Unknown
Decorator: Unknown
Capacity: 900
Opens: 31 December 1908
Closes: 5 September 1931 (fire)
Present use: Demolished

Cinema: Lyric
Address: Stephenson Road, Heaton
Architect: Marshall and Tweedy, Ncle
Builder: Thomas Clements & Sons, Ncle
Decorator: R J Richardson, Ncle
Capacity: 1594
Opens: 6 January 1936
Closes: 20 June 1959
Present use: theatre

Cinema: Lyric
Address: Newburn Road, Throckley
Architect: Percy L Browne and Glover, Ncle
Builder: Unknown
Decorator: Unknown
Capacity: 850
Opens: 15 May 1935
Closes: 8 October 1966
Present use: Demolished, 1992

Cinema: Majestic
Address: Condercum Road, Benwell
Architect: Dixon and Bell, Ncle
Builder: Unknown
Decorator: Unknown
Capacity: 1,400
Opens: (3 Oct 1927 as theatre); 4 Aug 1930
Closes: 20 May 1961
Present use: Demolished May 2004

Cinema: Minerva (later Imperial)
Address: 127 Byker Bank
Architect: A P Farthing, Ncle
Builder: Unknown
Decorator: Unknown
Capacity: 437 (300 stalls, 137 circle)
Opens: ? 15 August 1910
Closes: 24 August 1963
Present use: Demolished, 1985

Cinema: New Westgate (later Gaumont)
Address: Westgate Road/Clayton Street
Architect: Percy L Browne and Sons, Ncle
Builder: Unknown
Decorator: Unknown
Capacity: 1,870 (1145 stalls, 725 circle)
Opens: 31 October 1927
Closes: 29 November 1958
Present use: Carling Academy

Cinema: Newcastle (later Grey Street)
Address: 10-12 Grey Street
Architect: White and Stephenson, Ncle
Builder: George Douglas, Ncle
Decorator: Unknown
Capacity: 927 (719 stalls, 208 circle)
Opens: 6 May 1914
Closes: 14 May 1932
Present use: Bank

Cinema: News Theatre
Address: Pilgrim Street
Architect: George Bell (Dixon and Bell), Ncle
Builder: Thomas Clements & Son., Ncle
Decorator: Unknown
Capacity: 412 (252 stalls, 160 circle)
Opens: 1 February 1937
Closes: March 1968 (as News Theatre)
Present use: Tyneside Cinema

Cinema: Odeon
Address: The Gate, Newgate Street
Architect: Stephen Limbrick Associates, Glos
Builder: Sir Robert McAlpine
Decorator: Unknown
Capacity: 2,538 (1:436; 2:102; 3:273; 4:346; 5:130; 6: 160; 7:199; 8: 67; 9: 120; 10: 318; 11: 157; 12: 230
Opens: 27 November, 2002
Closes: Open 2005

Cinema: Olympia
Address: Northumberland Road
Architect: J Shaw, Ncle
Builder: Unknown
Decorator: W T Gibson, Gosforth
Capacity: 1,100 (352 stalls, 400 pit, circle 348)
Opens: 20 December 1909
Closes: 8 April 1961
Present use: Demolished, 1971

Cinema: Paramount (later Odeon)
Address: Pilgrim Street
Architect: Frank Verity & S. Beverley, London
Builder: Stanley Miller, Ncle
Decorator: C. Fox, Hollywood ('art director')
Capacity: 2,602
Opens: 7 September 1931
Closes: 26 November 2002
Present use: Vacant

Cinema: Pavilion
Address: Westgate Road
Architect: Wylson and Long, London
Builder: J. Parkinson & Sons, Ltd., Ncle
Decorator: F de Jong, London
Capacity: 1,585
Opens: (28 Dec 1903 theatre); 10 Dec 1917
Closes: 29 November 1975
Present use: Demolished, 1990-92

Cinema: Picture & Variety Palace (Imperial)
Address: Back Field Terrace, Throckley
Architect: Thomas Charlton, Newburn
Builder: ?T Charlton, Newburn
Decorator: Unknown
Capacity: 600 (estimated)
Opens: 12 November 1912 (licensing date)
Closes: 12 December 1922 (fire)
Present use: Demolished

Cinema: Picture House (later Westgate)
Address: Westgate Road/ Clayton Street
Architect: Arthur Stockwell, Ncle
Builder: Stephen Easten, Ltd., Ncle
Decorator: Unknown
Capacity: 850
Opens: 12 February 1912
Closes: 5 March 1927 (for rebuilding)
Present use: see Westgate

Cinema: Picture Palace (later Orion)
Address: Stamfordham Road, Westerhope
Architect: H F Burrows, Lemington
Builder: Unknown
Decorator: Unknown
Capacity: 450
Opens: 14 August 1912 (licensing date)
Closes: January 1970
Present use: Bingo club

Cinema: Picture Theatre
Address: Tyne View, Lemington
Architect: Thomas Gregory, Lemington
Builder: Unknown
Decorator: Unknown
Capacity: Unknown
Opens: 18 October 1911 (licensing date)
Closes: 3 March 1927 (licence refused)
Present use: burnt down, circa 1933

Cinema: Picturedrome and Variety Palace
Address: Spencer Rd/Westmacott St, Newburn
Architect: E Tweddle, West Hartlepool
Builder: E Tweddle, West Hartlepool
Decorator: Unknown
Capacity: Unknown
Opens: October 1910
Closes: 1911
Present use: Building moved to Throckley

Cinema: Picturedrome
Address: 36 Gibson Street/ Buxton Street
Architect: Hope and Tasker, Ncle
Builder: Millar and Besford, Whitley Bay
Decorator: J Thorne, Ncle
Capacity: 280 (209 stalls, 71 circle)
Opens: 30 July 1910
Closes: 20 August 1960
Present use: Demolished

Cinema: Plaza
Address: Westgate Road/Gowland Avenue
Architect: S J Stephenson, Ncle
Builder: H T and W A Smelt, Ncle
Decorator: Unknown
Capacity: 1247 (778 stalls, 469 circle)
Opens: 6 February 1928
Closes: 31 December 1960
Present use: Public House

Cinema: Prince of Wales
Address: Rokeby Street, Lemington
Architect: W J Clark, E Jackson
Builder: Straker Bros., Lemington
Decorator: Unknown
Capacity: 790 (534 stalls, 256 circle; stadium)
Opens: 14 July 1924
Closes: c.1960 (exact date unknown)
Present use: Demolished

Cinema: Queen's Hall
Address: Northumberland Place
Architect: Marshall and Tweedy, Ncle
Builder: Unknown
Decorator: Unknown
Capacity: 1413 (1047 stalls, 366 circle)
Opens: 9 September 1913 (public)
Closes: 15 June 1963
Present use: Converted to Cinerama Theatre

Cinema: Queen's Cinerama Theatre
(former Queen's Hall)
Address: Northumberland Place
Architect: Unknown
Builder: Stephen Easten, Ncle
Decorator: Decorative Plaster Co., Ncle
Capacity: 972 (613 stalls, 359 circle)
Opens: 9 November 1963
Closes: 16 February 1980
Present use: Demolished

Cinema: Raby
Address: Commercial Rd/Oban Rd, Byker
Architect: White & Stephenson, Ncle
Builder: Unknown
Decorator: Unknown
Capacity: 825 (195 stalls, 450 pit, 178 circle)
Opens: 17 January 1910
Closes: 7 March 1959
Present use: Demolished

Cinema: Regal
Address: Two Ball Lonnen, Fenham
Architect: J H Morton, South Shields
Builder: Hastie Burton Ltd., North Shields
Decorator: Fred A Foster Ltd., Nottingham
Capacity: 1226 (818 stalls, 408 circle)
Opens: 8 November 1933
Closes: 30 April 1960
Present use: Offices

Cinema: Regent (replaced Scotswood)
Address: Bridge Crescent, Scotswood
Architect: Robert Burke, Ncle
Builder: Unknown
Decorator: Unknown
Capacity: 536 (332 stalls, 204 circle); stadium
Opens: 29 December 1938 (licensing date)
Closes: 6 July 1957
Present use: Demolished, 1964

Cinema: Rex
Address: Ferguson's Lane, Benwell Village
Architect: S J Stephenson and Gillis, Ncle
Builder: H T Smelt, Ncle
Decorator: M Alexander and Sons., Ncle
Capacity: 1,012 (634 stalls, 378 balcony)
Opens: 8 December 1938
Closes: 10 August 1968
Present use: Social club

Cinema: Rialto
Address: Armstrong Road, Benwell
Architect: Percy L Browne, Son & Harding,
Ncle
Builder: Walter Wilson, Ltd., Ncle
Decorator: M Alexander and Sons, Ncle
Capacity: 1,026 (668 stalls, 358 balcony)
Opens: 10 May 1937
Closes: 25 June 1961
Present use: Demolished

Cinema: Royal (later Palladium)
Address: 17-19 Groat Market
Architect: F M Dryden, Ncle (conversion)
Builder: Unknown
Decorator: Unknown
Capacity: 963 (261 stalls, 305 pit, 397 circle)
Opens: 15 June 1908
Closes: 30 September 1939
Present use: Demolished

Cinema: Royalty
Address: High Street, Gosforth
Architect: Marshall and Tweedy, Ncle
Builder: William Hall, Ltd., Gateshead
Decorator: R J Richardson, Ncle
Capacity: 1,156 (790 stalls, 366 circle)
Opens: 17 October 1934
Closes: 30 December 1981
Present use: Demolished

Cinema: Savoy
Address: Westmorland Rd/Beech Grove Rd
Architect: SJ Stephenson Ncle (conversion)
Builder: H T Smelt, Ncle
Decorator: Fred A Foster Ltd., Nottingham
Capacity: 791
Opens: 12 December 1932
Closes: 29 May 1966 (fire)
Present use: Demolished

Cinema: Scala
Address: Chillingham Road, Heaton
Architect: Percy L Browne, Ncle
Builder: W Thompson, Ncle
Decorator: Unknown
Capacity: 1051 (560 stalls, 312 pit, 163 circle,
16 dress circle)
Opens: 10 March 1913
Closes: 1 July 1961
Present use: Demolished

Cinema: Scotswood
Address: Bridge Crescent, Scotswood
Architect: F M Dryden, Ncle (conversion)
Builder: Unknown
Decorator: Unknown
Capacity: 290
Opens: 1 April 1926
Closes: end 1938 (see Regent)
Present use: Demolished

Cinema: Star (later Apollo)
Address: Prudhoe Street
Architect: W H Knowles, Ncle (conversion)
Builder: Unknown
Decorator: Unknown
Capacity: 700 (est.)
Opens: 13 April 1908
Closes: 1914 (exact date untraced)
Present use: demolished

Cinema: Stoll
Address: Westgate Road
Architect: W B Parnell, Ncle; F Matcham, London (for conversion)
Builder: J and W Lowery, Ncle
Decorator: J Richardson and Co., Ncle
Capacity: 1,370
Opens: 2 June 1919
Closes: 23 March 1974
Present use: Theatre/ concert venue

Cinema: Studios 1-4
Address: Waterloo Street
Architect: Unknown
Builder: Unknown
Decorator: Unknown
Capacity: 1:85; 2:112; 3:105; 4:142
Opens: 13 December 1973 26 March 1983
Present use: Converted to apartments, 2003-4

Cinema: Sun
Address: Long Row, Byker Hill (Shields Rd)
Architect: W R Storey, Gateshead (c'version)
Builder: Unknown
Decorator: Unknown
Capacity: 350 (250 stalls, 100 balcony)
Opens: 29 November 1909
Closes: after 2 February 1934
Present use: Demolished

Cinema: Tatler News Theatre
Address: 149 Northumberland Street
Architect: J Newton Fatkin, Ncle
Builder: Unknown
Decorator: Fred A Foster Ltd., Nottingham
Capacity: 437; stadium type
Opens: 16 December 1937
Closes: 24 August 1980
Present use: Demolished

Cinema: Tivoli
Address: Walker Road/Raby Street
Architect: Unknown
Builder: Unknown
Decorator: Unknown
Capacity: circa 250
Opens: pre-18 July 1908
Closes: circa 1912
Present use: Demolished

Cinema: Vaudeville
Address: Church Street, Walker
Architect: White and Stephenson, Ncle (1908 theatre); J Johnson, Hebburn (1910 picture hall)
Builder: T M Miller, Whitley Bay
Decorator: Unknown
Capacity: 390; stadium type
Opens: 23 November 1908
Closes: 2 August 1958
Present use: Demolished

Cinema: Walker Picture House (later Regal)
Address: Church Street, Walker
Architect: Edwin Liddle, Ncle (conversion)
Builder: Unknown
Decorator: Unknown
Capacity: 650
Opens: ? April 1910 (but see text)
Closes: 28 Feb 1949 (licence not renewed)
Present use: Demolished

Cinema: Warner
Address: Manors
Architect: Ira Steigler, Howard & Unick
Builder: P Whelan
Decorator: Unknown
Capacity: 3386 (1: 404; 2: 398; 3: 236; 4: 244; 5: 290; 6: 659; 7: 509; 8: 398; 9: 248
Opens: 8 December 1989
Closes: 16 April 2004
Present use: Demolished

Cinema: Welbeck
Address: Scrogg Road/Byker Street
Architect: J Newton Fatkin, Ncle
Builder: Unknown
Decorator: Unknown
Capacity: 965 (360 stalls, 290 pit, 315 circle)
Opens: 4 November 1929
Closes: after 6 December 1968
Present use: Bingo club

NOTE: Capacity figures for individual cinemas vary over the years, affected by changes in type and spacing of seating.

THE END OF THE ROAD

E·H·GRIFFITHS' PRODUCTION

◆

A PHOTO PLAY THAT TELLS A STORY OF LIFE ALL OUGHT TO KNOW—ALL WILL WANT TO SEE

Credits

I would like to record my thanks to all those who have helped in the writing of this book, by agreeing to be interviewed, by writing to me with information following a letter in the *Evening Chronicle* and in many other ways. The greatest pleasure of the work for me has been the unstinting help received from all those now or formerly in the business. Any errors or faulty interpretations in the book are my responsibility.

John Airey, M Aynsley and Sons Ltd., Tom Bainbridge, John Barnes, Muriel Bell, George Belshaw, Doug Bond, the British Film Institute, the British Library Newspaper Library, Jill Brown, Ken Brown, Richard Brown, John Browne, Douglas Buglass, Robert Bullivant, Robert A Burke, Ronnie Callaghan, Eric Caller, Terry Charnock, the Cinema Theatre Association, Gordon Clark, Tom Clark, Christopher Clavering, Thomas Clements and Sons Ltd., Mrs L Coulson, Ian M Dawe, Edward Dietz, Tom Dixon, Con Docherty, Peter Douglas, K Douglass, Stephen Easten Ltd. (Mr Sutherland), Alfred E Finlay, Andy Forster, Douglas Gibson, Joe Ging, Mervyn Gould, clients of the Grange Day Centre, Throckley, Glyn Hall, Margaret Hall, Noel Hanson, Percy Harding, David Hinge, Elizabeth Hodges, John Hodgson, Geoff Hornsby, Maria Hoy, Mrs W Huggins, Robert Hutton, Les Irwin, Mr Johnson, Dr A Jones, Pat Jones, Mrs Lear, G A Lewins, Michael Long, Joan Lowery, John McMahon, Joe Marsh, Geoff Mellor, Mr Miller, Bob Milner, Mannie Moorhouse, Tony Moss, Paul Mustard, Newcastle Chronicle and Journal Ltd, Fred Norris, Ethel Oakley, Audrey Patterson, Keith Proctor, the Rank Organisation (Percy Aruliah), Bill Rosser, Elizabeth Sewell, John Sharp, Trish Sheldon, Bob Spurs, Bill Stewart, Vincente Stienlet, Sunderland Central Library (Local Studies), Peter Talbot, Bill Taylor, Mike Thomas, Neil Thompson, Bill Travers, Turners Photography, Tyne and Wear Archives Department, Des Walton, Warner Cinemas, Bill Whitehead, Dave Wilmore, Mr and Mrs G W Wilkinson.

I would like especially to thank John Matthews and the Northumberland and Newcastle Society for the use of their superb set of Paramount photographs.

Index of cinemas and people